Driftwood and Tangle

Driftwood and Tangle

Margaret Leigh

BIRLINN

This edition published in 2010 by
Birlinn Limited
West Newington House
10 Newington Road
Edinburgh
EH9 1QS

www.birlinn.co.uk

ISBN: 978 1 84158 898 8

British Library Cataloguing-in-Publication Data
A catalogue record for this book is available from the British Library

Designed by James Hutcheson
Typeset by Hewertext UK Ltd, Edinburgh
Printed and bound by CPI Cox & Wyman Ltd, Reading

Contents

Introduction

Margaret Mary Leigh (1894–1973) was her own man. The daughter of an Oxford don, reared by her mother with the help of a governess, she thought nothing of shifting dung, binding sodden sheaves or cursing at cattle. Perhaps the most truthfully footloose of a generation of writers on the Great Highland Outdoors, her specialities were manual labour and minute observation of nature. She had no desk or study but some kitchen table which was seldom her own. Her writing was done on winters' nights to the whisper of a Tilley lamp. And here in *Driftwood and Tangle* it is at its most experimental. The title may be couthy, but, as usual with her, it hides a great deal. Writing like an unsentimental angel, she imparts thoughts, memories, opinions, experiences, sounds, sights and smells to a piece of paper. It is not topographical or historical writing, nor is it natural history or an account of the agricultural year, though there are elements of all these things in it, along with the odd touch of folklore and literary criticism. In each of these two dozen essays she is trying something a little bit different. Writing about herding cattle, say. Or snow. Or truth, lies and half-truths. Or just writing hot from the general stores of a richly stocked mind to see where it takes her.

We, too, wonder where she will take us, and that is Leigh

at her best. But always she comes back to the Highlands, for that is where she is, and that is the place she loves above all others. So, to put the thing briefly, this is a delightful and individualistic book about certain places as they were in the 1930s and early 1940s: Fernaig in South West Ross, the isle of Tanera further north, Morvern, Moidart and Barra, with a visit to Eriska in Argyll.

Margaret Leigh was, I believe, a first cousin of the novelist Dorothy Leigh Sayers. She was born at 149 Harley Street, London, on 17 December 1894. Her father was Henry Devenish Leigh, a fellow and tutor of Corpus Christi College. In 1891 he had married another classical scholar, Alice Maud Bayliss, daughter of a Birmingham ironmaster, a student of the women's college, Somerville. Margaret's elder brother had died at birth, so she was an only child. Her father fell sick, and, in the way of the time, was advised to go in search of a more salubrious climate. So it was that the family, little Margaret included, found itself wandering from hotel to hotel in Egypt and the Tyrol. Perhaps this is what turned her into a restless wanderer of our rainy western shores who liked to put down deep roots in the soil before pulling them up again. Her father died at Lucerne in 1903 when she was eight, and one of her abiding memories became the 'pang I felt in childhood when, with nose pressed against the nursery pane, I heard the fading clip-clop of the hansom that bore my mother away to a party'.

The rest of Margaret's youth consisted of helping her mother in the struggle to preserve respectability while making ends meet, education at Oxford High School, holidays at Wells, in the Fens, or (on one occasion) Switzerland, and coping with a curvature of the spine which afflicted her at the age of twelve: 'as a child I spent a winter in Cornwall, perched on a high ridge above Fowey harbour'. She became enthusiastic about poetry, music, wild nature and Plato, in that order. It is clear from her books which of these won out, and the reason was simple enough, for a holiday trip to Shetland in her teens imprinted dramatic images on her brain which were never forgotten.

In 1913 Margaret won a classical scholarship to Somerville, but while at college her interests drifted towards philosophy, ancient history, spirituality, the nature of existence and the role of women. Her holidays with her mother continued: Rome, Florence. Reared an Anglican, she discovered the gospel of St John, thought for the first time of becoming a Catholic, left the Church of England in 1916, and became a Quaker. While developing an admiration for asceticism and virginity, and forming a personal theology of salvation through single-minded devotion to work, she fell in love with a woman – Platonic, of course. 'Marriage for its own sake,' she once wrote, 'meant nothing to me. The physical side repelled me, for my own enlightenment had come from the secret study of forbidden passages in the classics.'

In 1917 she took a government job in London, followed rapidly by one in Oxford. It was a time of change for women. The war gave them opportunities, the peace added powers and freedoms. All of these she embraced wholeheartedly. She rediscovered Cornwall, was courted by John, became engaged to him in 1918, broke it off, took a job in Scotland as classics mistress at St Leonard's School in St Andrews, and left the Quakers. Her personal problem was that she was the wrong age at the wrong time. Having had no interest in boys before the war when they were 'as plentiful as blackberries', she found that 'when I did begin to quest vaguely for a mate, the men of my generation were dead'. But the shortage of males (and her own work ethic) stood her in good stead professionally, and in 1919 she was appointed to a lectureship in Classics at Reading University.

Though close to her mother once again, she did not enjoy her new situation for long. The college was riddled with factionalism, and women were tolerated rather than encouraged. She immersed herself in Thomas Hardy and the Brontë sisters, who, as she is at pains to point out to us in a footnote to *Driftwood and Tangle*, were not English at all, but Irish on one side and Cornish on the other. The astonishingly long academic vacations of those days allowed her to spend twenty-two weeks of the year in a cottage at Zennor in 1921–22, and 'the creature that came out of Chyreen was very different from the one that went in'. She experienced a profound sense of eternity, turned with enthusiasm to Celtic Studies and to creative writing, found an outlet in the *Hibbert Journal*, and produced first a little book of poems (*Songs from Tani's Garden*, 1923), then, in 1924, her first novel. Called *The Passing of the Pengwerns*, it won a long review in *The Times Literary Supplement*, sold less than 300 copies, and earned what she ruefully described as 'the price of a good litter of farrows'.

Margaret was determined to become a successful

writer, however, and these were mere rites of passage. As if in a Brontë novel, what really counted at this point was a legacy. It allowed her to throw in her lecturing job, buy a cottage in a place where she really wanted to be – Plockton in Wester Ross, which combined West Highland scenery with the advantages of a railway station. In 1925, when she was thirty, she and her mother went to live there.

Complete freedom had at last arrived. For the first time in her life Margaret began to experience sexual desire, and was in a mood to accept marriage were it offered, but she had brought herself to a place where no suitable mate was likely to manifest himself; she became 'hard, restless, cynical', and when her second novel, *Love the Destroyer*, met with modest success, she went out and bought a rowing boat.

It had become clear that writing on its own was going to bring neither spiritual satisfaction nor regular income. The only industry in Plockton capable of providing employment for a woman was agriculture, and she began in 1928 by studying the subject to diploma level for three terms at Oxford. She must have met John Lorne Campbell, eleven years her junior, who was doing the full Oxford University course in agriculture at the time, and went on to become a celebrated Gaelic scholar, folklorist and laird of Canna. Her study of the history of land use in the Highlands from 1790 to 1883 was published across fifty-six pages of *The Scottish Journal of Agriculture* for 1928 and 1929, but in the Christmas vacation she worked on a dairy farm near Oxford, and in the Easter vacation on the 6,000-acre sheep-farm at Fernaig, a few miles up the Loch Carron shore from Plockton.

Fernaig is better known to university students of Gaelic as
a manuscript than as a farm, for it was the name given to a
collection of poems made by Duncan MacRae of Inverinate,
an enthusiastic Episcopalian and Jacobite, during the years
1688–93, which fell into the possession of the Mathesons of
Fernaig, and lies today in Glasgow University Library. But
Margaret was busy losing her appetite for such things. She
was employed as a farm-hand at Fernaig for the next four
years, except in 1930 when she seized the opportunity of a
lifetime to bring a party of boys to Fairbridge Farm School
in Western Australia. In 1932, at the age of thirty-seven, she
became engaged for the second time, but the man broke it
off. It was for the best, she later reflected: 'I was much too
impatient and selfish to carry a double burden.'

In 1933 Margaret obtained the tenancy of a small farm
called Achnadarroch, between Fernaig and Plockton (in
Highland Homespun Achnadarroch is 'Achnabo' and Fernaig
is 'Strathascaig'). Her first idea was to use it as a temporary
home for Poor Law children who would go on to Fairbridge.
Although the scheme was encouraged by the Child Emigration
Society, it had to be abandoned because the authorities would
not send children to a district beyond the normal reach of
their inspectors. She thus avoided innocent involvement in a
massive programme of child exploitation and abuse which has
been documented in David Hill's book *The Forgotten Children:
Fairbridge Farm School and its Betrayal of Britain's Child Migrants to
Australia*, and for which the prime minister of Australia made
a public apology in 2009.

Margaret became consumed, as she said herself, by a

'stoic devotion to manual work as a cure for the maladies of the soul and for the disquietudes of the heart'. She worked twelve, fourteen, sixteen hours a day, liberated and fed by natural beauty, but the inevitable happened. She fell in love with her assistant, whom she called 'David' in *The Fruit in the Seed*, and 'Peter' in *Highland Homespun* and *Spade among the Rushes*. 'Peter' was eighteen years old.

After only two years at Achnadarroch the proprietor refused to renew the lease. The couple considered farming the Crowlin Isles, or taking a croft near Dunvegan, but in the summer of 1935, by which time Margaret had begun to write again, they took a small dairy farm called Newton (in Cornish 'Trenoweth') on the edge of Bodmin Moor. The three years in Cornwall proved to be the most difficult of her life – not surprisingly, given that *Highland Homespun*, her most successful book, was published in 1936, and David left her in 1937, the year of *Harvest of the Moor*, the first few chapters of which are actually about the Highlands.

Margaret had discovered the hard way that the key to good writing is personal experience. Giving up Newton, she accepted a commission to travel on horseback from Bodmin to the Scottish border. This she did in September–October 1938. The result was *My Kingdom for a Horse*, which in an evil moment she was tempted to call *England No More*. Typically, one of the reasons she gives for making the journey is this: 'I wanted to learn the technique of long-distance horseback travelling under easy conditions in a civilised country, and then see whether I had sufficient strength and resource to do the same thing in wilder places.' As she tells us in *Spade among the Rushes*, she fulfilled the latter ambition a few years afterwards when she rode in continuous rain from Smirisary to Fernaig through the entire Rough Bounds of the Highlands.

After returning to Scotland in October 1938 Margaret visited her friends in Fernaig and Morvern, travelled to Ireland with her mother, then went on to Barra and South Uist. She put the finishing touches to *My Kingdom for a Horse* in North Uist in March. Back home in Plockton, she wrote a novel, *The Further Shore*, which was never published. There were to be no more novels: reality suited her best. In August 1939 she went to spend some time on Tanera in the Summer Isles with the pioneering English ecologist Frank Fraser Darling and his wife Marian ('Bobbie'), who were farming there. It is perhaps a little curious that in her two essays on Tanera in *Driftwood and Tangle* she fails to mention the outbreak of the Second World War, but that is Margaret Leigh – never predictable.

With mobilisation in autumn 1939 it was easy for her to return to her old job as a farm labourer at Fernaig. She began to learn Gaelic, and her thoughts on that subject are to be found in Chapter 20 below. She is slightly economical with the truth, however. There were plenty of monoglot Gaelic speakers in those days, not least in Barra, where she went in the winter of 1940–41 to finish *Driftwood and Tangle* and continue her studies, living in a furnished cottage with a dog for company. Perhaps her real problem was that in wartime mysterious strangers, even (or especially?) female ones, were assumed to be spies.

From the Barra perspective the title *Driftwood and Tangle* was obvious enough for a miscellaneous collection of essays, four of which (Chapters 6, 14, 15, 24) had appeared in the *Glasgow Herald*, and two (Chapters 7, 10) in the *Guardian*. Margaret was beachcombing her life, never quite sure what she would stumble over, or even slip on, in the *tiùrr* of her own thoughts (she uses the word in Chapter 17). The book was duly published in 1941, and in Chapter 5 we discover her trajectory: she was back on the road to Rome. She herself felt on re-reading *Highland Homespun, Harvest of the Moor* and *Driftwood and Tangle* that her 'nature-mysticism was not static: it had its joyful spring, its deeper and more sombre maturity, and its troubled, uncertain decline'. She claimed to find 'a note of sadness, almost of disillusion' in *Driftwood and Tangle*, and by way of example she cites her remarks on sorrow in Chapter 1, and also Chapter 21, which she describes as a commentary on Conrad's saying that 'the most amazing wonder of the deep is its unfathomable cruelty'. But this woman was not running away. 'My ancient passion for solitude and wild nature grew and deepened,' she recalled, 'until, at the beginning of the last war, it became the dominant influence in my life.'

That is why Margaret Mary Leigh's road to Rome lay through a croft at the back of beyond: to be precise, in the decaying township of Smirisary behind Glenuig in Catholic Moidart. Her farming friends in Morvern, Graham Croll and his mother, helped her obtain it. Her personal cross was 'a spade in the rushes', and although there is probably more humour in the book of that name than in anything else she wrote, it was laughter in the face of the devil, for by now the land was irredeemable. Her mother died (at Auchterawe House near Fort Augustus) in 1944, and she wrote Spade among the Rushes in 1946–47; it was published in 1949, and reprinted in 1974 and 1996.

Margaret was admitted into the Catholic Church in 1948; her revised edition of *Highland Homespun* appeared in the same year, and was reprinted in 1974. She went back to Oxford, took her vows as a Carmelite nun, entered a convent in 1950, and wrote her autobiography, *The Fruit in the Seed*, which was published in 1952. Her extraordinary choice of an enclosed order was as misguided as her choice in men. When she died at 1a Leachkin Road in Inverness on 7 April 1973, her address was 2 Aultgrishan, Gairloch, in Wester Ross.

In Chapter 6 Leigh risks a caricature which will help us define her place in literature. 'There seems to be a ceaseless demand,' she says, 'for books and articles written to a familiar recipe – a few sea birds, a handful of wild flowers, the sun setting in the western ocean, a legend or two, an anecdote of the '45, and a few tags of Gaelic.' This does not describe her work, but it helps us understand why a book in which the author is careful to point out that clothes were obtained by mail order came to be called *Highland Homespun*. She was operating on the edge of a crowded field. T. Ratcliffe Barnett (1868–1946) was a distinguished Presbyterian minister with an Edinburgh congregation, an open but mystical mind and a taste for walking who rattled off books with titles like *The Road to Rannoch and the Summer Isles*. M. E. M. Donaldson (1876–1958) was an Englishwoman with a talent for photography and an interest in Jacobitism who preferred 'wanderings' to 'roads', perhaps to emphasise that she was off Barnett's well-beaten track: *Further Wanderings, Mainly in Argyll*, for example. Leigh's caricature does scant justice to Seton Gordon (1886–1977), an Oxford-educated member of an old Aberdeenshire family who was an excellent writer, an ornithologist, and almost as good an observer of wild nature as herself. 'Roads' and 'wanderings' being used up, his best-loved books bear titles like *Highways and Byways in the West Highlands*. (To be fair, 'Highways and Byways' was a long-established Macmillan series.)

Recalling how she had considered taking a croft in Skye, Leigh wrote that 'we might have come to live in the Celtic twilight and write like Fiona Macleod or Mr Alasdair Alpin Macgregor'. The career of Mr Macgregor (1899–1970) was in a sense the reverse of her own: the son of a doctor, travel-writer and Gaelic poet from Stornoway, he lived in London but made annual photographic forays through the Highlands, and produced a stream of folklore-based books with titles like *The Peat-Fire Flame*, culminating in some insensitive remarks in *The Western Isles* (1949) which earned him the loathing of almost everyone he had ever written about. It is no coincidence that Leigh's best friend among the many writers on the Highlands was Frank Fraser Darling (1903–79), whose natural successor as a student of nature conservation was John Morton Boyd (1925–98). By the 1960s, however, the most popular books on the Highlands were being written by an upper-class homosexual, Gavin Maxwell (1914–69), about economic disasters and exotic animals, while readers with quieter tastes were generally content with *The Scots Magazine*. The Highlands themselves were no longer exotic; with the foundation of the Highlands and Islands Development Board, people ceased to speak of 'the Highland Problem', and as there was no longer felt to be a problem, books like Leigh's were no longer consulted for solutions. Ironically, it is books like Leigh's which, being entirely contemporary in their own day, have now gained historical value as first-hand portraits of her time. Unlike Darling, Leigh has her eye firmly fixed upon the general reader; unlike Donaldson, she never misrepresents folklore or clothes the past in inappropriate sentiments.

For a work of recent history to survive it must be appealingly written as well as authentic. In this respect Leigh's essays in *Driftwood and Tangle* are second to none. As I have said, we never know which way she will go. 'The Day is Far Spent' is a 'road' (or 'wanderings'?) essay about a walk to Kyle, but she is ambushed by her own thoughts and only seems to get as far as Duirinish. 'The Solitary Reaper' is an account of a single day to rival Ulysses, but one would never know it from its Wordsworthian title. 'Thy People Shall Be My People' turns out to be on Irish nationalism. 'At the Peats, June 1940' sounds so like a poem that it is almost a surprise to discover that peats and the awful events of 1940 are very much her subject. 'Why Haste Ye to Rise Up So Early?' is about the Highland reputation for sloth. 'Hand to Mouth, the Best Portion' is an essay on class which begins with blackbirds/people and moves on through tinkers/crofters and captains/kings to the wonderful levellings in Campbell's

Popular Tales of the West Highlands. Says Leigh: 'There is something intriguing in the thought of the High King's daughter tramping the glens with her load of bowls for sale. The storyteller saw nothing unseemly in it, and neither need we.'

Ronald Black

January 2010

A Word to the Reader | 1

Many things are cast up on the shore, but only those that have been first given to the sea; and this book has more unity than its title might suggest. Every chapter but one deals with things seen and done and thought about in the Western Highlands and Islands of Scotland. All were written since the outbreak of war, while I was working on a neighbour's farm in Wester Ross, or helping other friends in Morvern and in Coigeach, or spending the dark slack weeks of mid-winter in the isle of Barra. This I have tried to make clear in the course of the book, but it is not really important.

For the chapters that follow are informal, like fireside conversations, and are chiefly meant for people like myself, with an empty chair at the other side of the hearth. Wild Nature will never betray its lovers; and for those who have no lively religious faith, it alone can mend the broken heart. But the price may be heavy. The love of Nature, once it becomes a passion, can be as estranging as the sea itself. He who follows it far becomes apart, as if, like the seal-people, he lived a hidden life elsewhere. And that other life has as much in it of sorrow as of joy.

Literature, not merely for information or distraction, but as a thing of beauty in itself, must be carried on at all costs. The writer's gear is cheap enough, God knows, and if we cannot get into print, we must imitate the ragged Irish poets of the eighteenth century, and spread ourselves by recitation and the copying of manuscripts. Monks, working among the smoking ruins of sacked libraries, kept literature and learning alive through Europe's first dark night. We in the second can hardly do less. It may not after all be so wicked to fiddle while Rome burns: it all depends on the tune and the ears that hear it. And at long last, when all the pens are broken and fiddles dumb, there will still be waves breaking on the long sands of the Western Isles.

ALLASDALE, ISLE OF BARRA
February 1941

In these high latitudes winter is measureless, all-powerful in its extremes of storm or of calm. Gales come, savage and shattering, day after day without respite. Then suddenly the wind falls, the sea goes down, and the whole world sleeps for a while. Of the sundering noise of wind I need say little here. Anyone who has lain sleepless through the long night, listening to the blast shrieking through bare branches, crashing impotently against the rocky walls of the glens, will know without telling. In that vast uproar, the individual with his burden of private thoughts and hopes is alone, submerged, like a drifting waterlogged hulk. Here as I sit by myself in December, at Allasdale on the west coast of Barra, with the gale's uproar drowning the thunder of waves, I seem as far from my neighbours as if the strip of machair between us were the whole desert of Arabia. I am already bound by a deepening sense of apartness, of detachment, always so strong in small islands. It is as if your little world were attached to the big one over there by a thread that might at any moment break, and set it adrift in space, alone with wandering hosts of stars. And it wouldn't matter. At first we think about mails, and curse if the steamer misses a call. And then we settle down, and would not care if she never came at all.

Thus are we englobed in our private world of storm. Then one morning the sun comes out of a quiet sea, and we open our tightly barred windows and doors to the unlooked-for brightness of day. And this is the other extreme of winter – its unbelievable silence and peace.

This silence of winter is most deeply felt in the glens, where every small noise, especially those made by man, are echoed and magnified till they acquire the sudden, almost frightening quality of a stone dropped into a black lochan of the hills. For the lesser sounds of the wild – leaves rustling, or song of birds or drone of bees – are all hushed: and if there is no wind, even the branches are still, and there is nothing to hear but the burns, which in dry and frosty weather are themselves muted or silent.

In the strange winter of 1939–1940 we had many such days. People began to say that the Highland climate was changing, as it must have changed even in historical times, when (it is supposed) increasing wind and rain put an end to the forests. But now the old order has been restored and we can only think that last winter was a 'pet day' on a large scale. Day after day we would watch the sun, with rays level and glowing, slant across a shoulder into the glen, leaving the southern side in cold blue shadow, for from the end of November till the middle of January no sun falls on our own land. We could see the northern side basking in that bright and transient warmth, like the sight of others' happiness when one's own is gone. Often a drift of sheep would come down a cleft in the hill, with a slanting beam from behind to put a bright edge round them. Everything, however small, that stood in the sun's path acquired an incredible depth and richness of colouring, especially where objects were dark in themselves, like the crimson-purple of birch stems and twigs, the violet of alder catkins, the rich glow at the heart of a black cow's winter coat, the tawny redness of a bundle of oat-sheaves thrown down for cattle. White, also, whose essential whiteness is intensified in twilight or under the cold sheen of moon and stars, receives an alien glow from a sun low in the heavens. Often we saw the dazzling brightness of blown spray, or of gulls following a boat, and a rosy light on the snow of the highest hills. On days of broken cloud there would be travelling gleams on the slopes, moving pools of light, like those cast by the head-lamps of a car. And one bright day in February, when I was rowing close under a little cliff, I saw the quivering play of ripples reflected on the smooth face of the rock.

All that winter we were busy with wood. Birches on the braes were cut in scores and thrown down to the road to be carted home at leisure. A great stillness lay over everything, in which the shriek of the saw, the ringing blows of the axe, and the splintering crash of falling trees, reverberated among the rocks, drowning the lap of water on stone, and the croon of eider-duck far out among the skerries. Then we would get the cart, and at nightfall come home with our load. There is something hypnotic about walking beside a cart. The noise of the wheels, continuous and almost as impersonal as the roaring of surf, travels with you, intimate as your shadow, englobing you in the world of your own thoughts. It is almost like walking in a high wind on the endless sands of South Uist. This noise of cart-wheels, when heard afar at the darkening, is one of the most poignant, the most evocative of human sounds, carrying our thoughts across ages and continents to the very heart of work and its end at the door of home. For all men's labour involves the moving of things in space, of which wheels are symbolic; and night, which brings all things home, gives a special blessing to the cart and its harsh and homely music.

I shall not easily forget a still November evening in West Kerry, when I stood on a high point of Valentia Island, watching the lonesome twilight look come over the hills of the mainland. To the north, across Dingle Bay, was Brandon, the second highest mountain in Ireland, with a wisp of cloud streaming from its summit. Westward, the heaving, wrinkled circle of the sea stretched luminous and unbroken from the Great Blasket to the Skelligs. The little stony fields were cleared of all crops, and men to whom time is nothing were shifting stones from gaps to let cows out or asses in. The boreens were full of wandering geese and turkeys, soon to be shipped from Cork to make an English Christmas. Small sounds fell like pebbles or raindrops into the pools of silence; but dominating all was the distant grinding of the ungreased axles of ass-carts bringing home load upon load of turf. Owing to the low price of asses, which is within the reach of all but the poorest, carts are far commoner in Ireland than in the Highlands, and their noise almost as friendly as the smell of the turf they carry.

The Atlantic may sleep, but it is never still. From every shore and skerry rose a vast continuous sighing, as if all strife and passion had died into acquiescence, into that acceptance of what is 'appointed' that seems to be the ultimate wisdom of the wild. The rocky field, the windswept hill has little profit to offer; but the harder its conquest, the greater its demand on patience and labour, the more passionately is it loved. As a man in Valentia, speaking of his croft, said to me: 'There isn't much money in it, but we have our health and enough to eat, and isn't that a great thing?'

But that was before the war. In the winter of 1940 we were too busy with our own wood-cutting to watch other people at work. I was returning for the last load, standing up in the cart, and singing at the top of my voice, for the wheels provided a pleasant accompaniment. There was a touch of frost in the air, just enough to stiffen the clothes I had laid out on the bleach, and to put a film of ice on the puddles, through which the wheels cut with a high-pitched crackle. The sky was faintly dappled with soft cloud, and in the misty air the hills of Applecross looked twice their real height. Snow lay along the horizontal ridges, marking the lines of stratification. By the time I had lifted the logs and roped the load, night was well on its way. The pines below the road rose straight into the air, without a movement, without a sigh. The tide was far out, and at the mouth of the river a wide delta of sand and mud spread fanwise, with gulls sitting in long ordered rows. After an unusually dry autumn there was not much water coming down the glen. The river murmured softly round the big stepping stones that led across to our cornfield with its well-thatched stack. Until Christmas is over, it is not easy to look on a cleared field without a keen memory of past labours – the heat and the midges, and those breathless thundery days when we waited for war.

In one way the war may prove a blessing in disguise. Like a long hard winter, it has barred the gates of the Highland fortress, and checked the infiltration of alien, standardising influences. But it has taken away our lights. When night falls the crofts are blind, the world of men lies dead till morning. People creep round the byres with shaded lamps and furtive torches. And it is a great missing, for the friendly reddish glow of a paraffin lamp, even the sheen of a lone candle in a naked window, is nowhere more welcome than in the empty spaces of the wild. Townsmen, robbed of the glare of their countless illuminations, can, if they choose, look up and see the stars, as souls who have lost all see God. But to us, who are always under the shadow of Nature's anger, the leaping wildfire, the brandished spears of the aurora may be too near for peace of mind, and the passionless gleam of stars above the snow may strip us of courage as well as of pride. We long for the unveiled lamp in a crofter's window, the fiery trail of the evening train, the serried lights of steamers bringing mails and food to the isles. And there are darker possibilities. One night in Barra a boy came in to see me, and we were talking about the crew of a ship's lifeboat. After nine days at sea, they had at last succeeded in getting ashore. But because of the black-out, these men, half dead and bewildered with their sufferings, were long unable to find a house, though there were plenty at hand. Thank God they have still left us the clear impartial gleam of our lighthouses.

Noctes orate serenas. Pray for calm nights of stars and clear sharp summits, with a deep glow beyond the horizon, and shafts of aurora bright enough to cast a shadow, faint but clearly perceptible, on the white hoar-frost underfoot. Nights when it is possible to open the house to the secret noises of the dark, and our minds to something beyond the beleaguered fortress of our solitude: when we are accepted members of the natural order, and not refugees, cowering under blankets from lightning and hail. Nights when it is pleasant to lie awake and watch the changing sky, till the stars grow pale in the east, and the first tremulous beam steals over the face of the waters.

And calm days too, when the short hours of sunshine are a long delight. On the last day of 1939 I went to the hill, and visited each of the lochs in turn. The ascent, being from the north side of the glen, lay cold in shadow. But as I neared the summit of the pass the level rays of the sun, in blinding brilliance, streamed through a gravelly cleft scooped out by the burn, and put a ring of glory round everything that stood in its path – rushes and tussocks of withered grass, and even blown hairs on the dog's back. The ground rang hard under my feet. Dry parchment-like bells of heather, bleached grass and sedges and canach stems stood rigid and still in the tightening grip of frost. Fragments of snow, which had melted and frozen again, lay in thin sheets of coarse crystal, very blue in the shadow, held up from below by mosses wiry with frost.

The long stretch of Loch na Gillean lay without ripple and empty, like water at the world's beginning. The trout we had harried all summer were at rest among the sleeping roots of lilies. At the eastern end, beyond the little beach of gravel, was an icefield about twelve feet wide and one inch thick. There had been hard frost three days before, followed by thaw with a strong west wind which, blowing down the length of the loch, had broken the outermost rim of ice and driven it back on itself; and the miniature pressure ridges thus formed had recently frozen again. Beyond this was a stealthy advance of young ice, ever expanding across the open water towards another tract of virgin film, delicately veined, like a drowned moth's wing. If a wind should rise and ruffle the water, the new-formed ice would break, and the tiny crystalline fragments jingle and chime with a musical note like nothing else in Nature. Sheep, looking unnaturally dark and dirty, moved away among patches of snow that crackled sharply under their feet. Bright clouds in the west were even more brightly reflected in the quiet levels of the loch. In the middle a stone lay dark against the sun, like the head of a beast swimming, to which a band of ripple, suddenly stirring, gave the illusion of movement. There was a strange contrast in the sky of opposite quarters. Westward, all was warm and bright with threads and feathers of gold. In the east was a grey emptiness from which would come the long night and the heavy hand of its frost.

How gladly now should we welcome a thaw, and exchange the glittering treasures of ice and snow for a puff of warm south wind! One morning we shall waken to feel a soft air, to hear the tinkle of water, the murmur of running streams. The immense, amazing icicles on the crags will begin to drip, and then to break in shattering fragments. The sheets of ice that cover, like armour plate, the face of a flat rock will start melting from the underside; and drops of water, darkly visible through the icy coating, will chase each other, like beetles or tadpoles, in hundreds and thousands. That will be a good day. For the West does not easily tolerate frost; it depletes the store of winter keep, and strains our nerves to cursing point. To see the edge of spring tides frozen, and hills white to sea level, as we did last year, is uncanny, disquieting. Better the roaring of wind, the breaking of waves, and tumult of burns; that is the kind of winter to which we are accustomed.

There is no month as dead as March, with its bleached rain-beaten grass and naked branches scarred with the storms of a whole winter. Yet as cocks will crow in the darkest hour before dawn, so there are days in March when spring seems nearer than our own bodies – soft days of calm, when the great stillness betrays the faintest stirrings of life. It was on such a day that I had been helping my friend in Morvern to dig his garden, and because the soil was soft and sticky after a night's rain, the end of day found us hot and rather tired. It was time for us to go for the cows, which had been driven to the hill to pick up what roughage they could, and thus save hay indoors. As we stood at the edge of the rise on which his steading was built, and looked across the flat fields at the head of Loch Teacuis, we spied a number of brown and white and black dots on the braes beyond those quiet waters, grazing high and in open formation, as cattle will in calm mild weather. There was no word of them turning home – indeed they seemed to contemplate a night out, which may have been a good sign at this season, but I can assure you that the sight gave us no pleasure. For to reach these happy grazings, the cattle had crossed the ebb at low water, and already the flowing tide had covered their tracks. We knew that if we had to take them round by the hill, we could never get them back before dark.

So we set out at once with sticks and dogs; and cutting across the bleached and sodden stubble, reached what was left of a narrow strip of shingle below the field fence. The tide was flowing with silent and barely perceptible speed – a stealthy brimming of steel-grey water. Loch Teacuis is a narrow, secluded inlet, one of those land-locked waters that only the tides and the seaweed claim for the sea. The hills about it are lonely and steep, and black in winter, for there is much rock and scree, and many a tract of soaking moss. At that time their gaunt sides were streaked with the foaming rush of torrents, for the rain had set every burn in spate, and a great roaring went up into the still air. Darkness was falling, but not very fast, for the lingering northern twilight makes itself felt as soon as we pass the equinox. The sky was covered with horizontal layers of soft cloud, parting in the west to reveal a tract of faintly gilded sky. The tide had already invaded the last strip of shingle between the enclosed fields and the hill.

The cattle – Highlanders, Galloways, and crosses, about forty-five head in all – still looked a long way off, and made no move to come home. We sent the dogs ahead to gather them, and after a while they came filing down to the loch-side, first the older cows, then the younger ones, and a jostling mob of stirks in the rear. By the time they reached the crossing-place, the cart ford and stepping-stones were covered by a gleaming sheet of water. The leaders looked and hesitated. At last, urged by shouts and barks and waving sticks, they entered the water, which in places reached belly-high and even to their shoulders, while the stirks were soon out of their depth and swimming for dear life. There was a mighty tossing of horns and a great splashing: yells and barks, re-echoing from above, ravished the peace of the hills. At last, on the home side of this improvised ford, we drove the herd across a wide boggy flat, where you must watch your feet in the gathering darkness. The flat, and the arable land above it, are cut in two by the river, which, being released from its narrow birchy gorge, rushed across the levels to the loch. This barrier was nothing to us or to the cattle; but the smaller of the two dogs, dashing in with careless zeal, was swept off his feet and rolled over and over downstream, till one of us darted down the bank and pulled him ashore. This dog has always been a philosopher. He shook himself over his rescuer, and then trotted off barking among the moving forest of legs.

It was quite dark when we reached the byre, where we hurried and stumbled with lanterns among stubborn beasts, trying to tie up the wide-horned Highlanders without damage to ourselves.

We were tired and hungry, but there was something about that trip that will always remain in my mind. The horns tossing like branches in storm, the splashing in the still water, the quiet levels of loch and sky, the roar of burns in the silence; and beyond all that, the realisation (in which lies the chief delight, and also the chief annoyance of herding) that the march of time is slowed down to the pace of the most deliberate member of the herd, so that you can dawdle, meditate, even dream with impunity, because you are doing a job both useful and necessary. For without you, the cattle would never go out to pasture nor come in to shelter. Without you, they would forever be where they should not, eating forbidden fruits, breaking fences, scattering, going astray. At the lowest, you may be merely keeping them company, for there are crofters' cows that will not settle to graze without human society.

As I sit now forlorn, with no cow of my own any more, and only my neighbours' beasts to study, how many memories of herding come back to me, memories of delight or exasperation, incidents funny, surprising, significant, or merely vexatious. At Fernaig there were times in autumn when the milk cows were allowed to graze for a certain period each day on the aftermath of hay already cut: and as there were in the same field unlifted potatoes and grass to be mown and hay still drying on fence or in coils, they could not be left alone without great risk. For no cow will settle for long on grass, however good, without poking her nose into something illicit, if only she gets the chance. Many an evening, when the milking was over, I would herd the cows for a while, till it became too dark to distinguish their forms except on the skyline. On calm nights I would come out in the open, leaning on the crook of a long stick, my vigil occasionally broken by a dash to wave one or other of them away from potatoes or standing grass. On nights of wind or driving showers, I would shelter in the lee of a big coil of hay and peer out from time to time to look at my charges, or to see if there were a fresh squall coming up from Applecross, or if the shower now pelting across the field were passing over, and a band of clear sky showing beyond the curtain of rain.

I was always tired, for I had been working since dawn. But it was good to get away from the voices and bright lights of the house, to be alone with the first stars.

Later, towards the end of September, when it was dark at milking time, I remember the harvest moon, round and full as no other moon in the year, rising above the jagged rim of the hills, and the cows moving east before me. I can see them now, passing one by one through the gate, and the moonbeams putting brightness on their rumps and hip bones and on the curving sides of their horns, and a halo round their soft hairy ears. And in the inky shadows of the buildings, how hard it was to distinguish the black heifer, who was always loitering in search of a bite of green grass from under the wall or a wisp of hay sticking out from the slats of the barn.

On the crofts, where crops are mostly unfenced, this herding may be somebody's full-time job, for cows unherded must be tied fasting in the byre, so that the longer you herd them outside, the more they will eat and the better their yield. It is a fine occupation for the aged, who can sit long hours in the sun, the old women knitting, and the old men smoking and watching the scene of past labours on land and sea. On quiet summer evenings when the midges are bad (and midges are the chief bane of the herdsman's life) they light a fire of sticks with perhaps a sod or two of peat to keep it going, and sit in the smoke. One evening when I crossed the moss to Portchuillin with a message to one of the crofters there, I found him at the herding with a woman of his township. The cows, three or four of them, were picking among the bog myrtle and heather, while the two crofters, who were not on specially friendly terms, kept a little distance apart, the woman knitting in the shelter of the peat stack, while the man, with smoke curling up from his pipe, was pottering round his, arranging and rearranging a few loose peats. Ewes were calling their lambs among birch and holly thickets on the steep braes, and from time to time a shower of stones came rattling down as a sheep crossed one of the many little screes that seamed the hillside. Westward the loch stretched out in quiet levels to Skye, broken in places by darkening bands of ripple. The tide made curling patterns in the narrows, and out beyond Reraig a porpoise came up to blow. This herding, and these herdsmen's fires reach back into a past beyond reckoning, and the sight of it, still there and still the same, brings comfort in a doomed and transient world.

The life of the herdsman, who keeps his sheep or his cattle, his camels or goats, on all the hills and plains, in all the desert places of the earth, is perforce solitary, and thus not far from the springs of spiritual life. He has nothing to hear but the cries of beasts and birds, the soughing of lonely winds, the mutter of distant thunder or moan of surf on the sands. He has nothing to watch but the slow rhythm of his grazing flocks, the march of the seasons, the changing face of the sky, and the mysterious pattern of his own soul. Old people at the herding have the endless web of their memories. But as this work is considered light and not specially skilled, it is often given to the very young; and for them the long lonely hours in the empty spaces are filled with dreams, and even with visions. It is not surprising that Joan of Arc and Bernadette Soubirous were both shepherdesses. No one who has read the *Story of an African Farm* will forget the lonely figure of Waldo, sitting on a kopje in the blinding noonday heat of the Karroo, watching his sheep and dreaming a boy's incommunicable dreams. The whole of this aspect of herding is summed up in Millet's picture of the shepherdess, leaning on her crook in the great plain, with evening sunbeams slanting across the backs of the sheep. A little way off is her dog, motionless, his eyes on the flock, waiting for the word of command that must come at last, however long delayed.

For sometimes, as we think, these young herdsmen must forget their flocks. Maybe for a time, but not for long. For there is an instinctive fidelity in herdsmanship which makes the shepherd willing to lay down his life for his flock, and a special significance in the injunction 'Feed my sheep'. So that your thoughts may wander for a while, even into Heaven, but only on a tether; and when pulled up, you will no doubt find your charges in some place where they should not be.

Then comes the jar, the sudden bump characteristic of life. Those who have never lived with animals or tended them are apt to underestimate their restlessness. A free herd is always on the move. Grazing is not omnivorous but selective, so that beasts do better on free range, even if with poorer pasture than in confinement on the best of grass. If you put hungry cattle into a good field, they will immediately fall on the grass near the gate; but they will not stay there long, nor will they graze systematically across a field. There is always much picking and choosing, as there is amongst humans when food is not too scarce. When full they will lie down to chew their cud; but after that, and sometimes before, they will roam wantonly in search of mischief. And what destruction can be done in a few minutes, if the herdsman's back is turned or his eyes closed! The veil of contemplation is rent from top to bottom, and he lays about him with a stick, shouting and cursing. The clumsy brutes, in bewilderment or sheer devilment, gallop hither and thither, while the dog, whom he trusts to do the right thing, mistakes his orders, and is worse than no dog at all.

The very nature and quality of a beast may, under some new stress, suddenly and unexpectedly change. There was at Fernaig a black heifer we called Zebo, because of the shining gloss of her summer coat. As a rule she was the quietest and most inoffensive of creatures. But there came a day when she had to be walked to the bull at Plockton, and a rope was put on her for the first time. We had Angus, our crofting neighbour, to lead her, and the Laird followed to see her safely across the ford. But when she reached the water, which was shallow enough, with a gravel bank in the middle, some devil entered into her, and she began to plunge and caper and rush about, with Angus trailing helplessly at the end of the long stout rope. The Laird tried to intervene, but was caught in the bight of the rope, and thrown head over heels into the mud on the farther bank. As he remarked himself, it took him some time to see the funny side of it.

To grown, active people, unless they happen to be gifted with unusual patience and good humour, the tending and herding of cattle is a tedious, exasperating business. But if you are interested in the individual characters and reactions of the herd, the whole thing is altered. Animal psychology is an almost virgin field, for our vision is so darkened by anthropomorphic prejudices that only by living with beasts, and in a manner shedding our own natures and assuming theirs, as certain shepherds and cowmen reckoned stupid in other ways will do by instinct, can we hope to gain insight into one of the world's most intriguing secrets. As every man in a crowd has a different face, a different character, so every sheep in a flock, every cow in a herd, has its own individual appearance and nature, which is well understood and distinguished by the experienced and sympathetic herdsman. The reactions of domestic animals, so much under the influence and control of man, are easier to study than those of wild creatures, where much remains a sealed book, except perhaps to those who are able and willing to enter so completely into animal lives that they almost cease to be human, except in their powers of sympathy and interpretation.

Perhaps I have left the reader with the impression that herding, when pursued by those with a few ideas to rattle in their heads, is no more than a cloak for idleness. There is really no need for such hypocrisy. For it is sometimes a good thing to be absolutely and shamelessly idle, not even to sit and think, but just to sit. And no man of thought and imagination can be blamed if he seeks some practical labour that can be combined with his own work without injury to either. And what better than work connected with the land, work in itself as old as man's life on earth and as inevitable as

death, and free from humbug and claptrap, from artificiality
and red tape and everything that stifles imagination and kills
the soul?

I have always mistrusted the purely literary fellow, the art-
for-art's-sake man. If you are an artist, you must certainly
practise art with your whole heart, even with ruthlessness if
need be. But he would be a poor creature who could not at
some time or other do some practical work as well, and make
a decent job of it. The world would be poorer if Sophocles
had never commanded a trireme at Salamis, if Conrad had
never handled a ship, if Lawrence of Arabia had written his
Seven Pillars without living it first. And to come to the present
time, and to a writer who has something cloistered and
academic about him – Charles Morgan. *The Flashing Stream*
is a fine play, whichever way you look at it, but it would lose
much of its power if the life and work of men engaged in
naval research were not shown from the inside, as by one
who had once shared it. It is impossible that such memories of young manhood, however vivid, should last for ever
undimmed; and unless they are renewed and replaced by
others, there is danger of resting on past achievement, which
too often ends in stagnation or even retreat.

It is a rare thing, and a fine one, to be able to plunge of
your own will into the hurly-burly, and share its life, without
surrendering the integrity of your spirit. During this second
winter of war, I saw a harbour, once crowded with yachts
and pleasure boats, given over to the grim traffic of war at
sea. The air was full of the drone of planes and flying-boats,
and the water churned up by naval trawlers, patrol boats,

and submarines. No place, you would think, for the life of
the wild. Yet on the wings of a flying boat a hundred gulls
were holding a parliament, as they might have done in the
wastes of ocean, on Suliskeir or Rona. Near them, perched
on a mooring-buoy, a cormorant sat in silent detachment.
Beside him floated two wild swans, white and remote as
if they were still on the farthest lochan of the isles. Thus,
through some tattered rift in the web of time, you may see
the ultimate peace.

Highlanders, like Irishmen, have often been accused of a disregard for truth. The problem is not as simple as it looks, since no one has been able to decide exactly what truth is. In this context it may mean fact, and especially brute fact; or it may mean that kind of devastating frankness which, when it occurs in a book, is praised by reviewers as 'sincerity'. The motive of this disregard may be either the desire to please the person you are talking to, or the wish to make a good story, the second being really an extension of the first, since the only function of a good story is to entertain its hearers. Now the desire to please may be caused by moral cowardice or love of gain, but a great deal of it is a survival of the immemorial hospitality of the wilderness. To be kind to the stranger, to let him down gently, to tell him things which, if not strictly accurate, will encourage him and fortify him in his journey, is an instinctive impulse, going back to the days when travellers in remote districts were rare enough to be taken for angels in disguise, or people in genuine distress, whose wants must be satisfied. All this, as a daily reality, has vanished, leaving only its afterglow in the hospitality which is still so marked in Highland life. But the modern car-borne traveller is too comfortable, transient, and self-sufficing to make a good guest; and in the State socialism we are plainly heading for, there will be no room for the poor and the compassion they excite.

Some of this courtesy is of course no more than ceremonial politeness, bearing little beyond its face value, which is received as it is offered. When Angus remarks that he has never seen the like of our bull (in any case a double-edged compliment), or when the shepherd tells me that I have more Gaelic than himself, they do not expect to be taken more seriously than the hostess who speeds the world's worst bore with an apparently heartfelt '*Must* you go?' These little insincerities oil the wheels of intercourse, and we notice their absence. I still remember with distaste a certain Lowland landlady who, when I came young and very shy to my first job in Scotland, asked, 'Why didn't you get a situation in your own country?' A perfectly fair question; but how glad I was to change my rooms, and take refuge with a Highland woman whose blankets were too short and armchairs broken, but who had the kindness and courtesy so often lacking where everything is in order, and the linoleum slippery as ice.

Now this is the social or kindly sort of lying. There is also the economy of truth practised by doctors, which is a professional matter, a form of faith-healing. And there is yet another kind, of which as a writer I am painfully and personally conscious: the manipulation of truth – or of brute fact, shall we say – for the sake of making a good story, to while away some dull or dismal hour. Boredom is one of mankind's worst enemies, and he who helps to defeat it should not be asked to verify his references. Fact in itself, like bare rock or naked bones, is always immensely interesting; but as seen through the dull blurred vision of most of us, it is like a glimpse of foggy landscape through a dirty window. To clean the glass may not always be possible; but to anyone with a quick mind and lively wit, the temptation to throw a few high-lights on the dim scene may prove irresistible. Naked we came into this world, and most certainly without the power of distinguishing between fact and fiction. It is the dreary business of nurses and teachers to hound us out of the world of romance and make-believe; and the more imaginatively gifted the child is, the more spanking or exhortation will be required, and the more is this faculty, with all its attendant blessings and curses, likely to persist into mature years.

In the childhood of the race it was the same. No one troubled to distinguish carefully between the deeds of gods and heroes and those of mortal men, or to draw a rigid frontier between visible and invisible. And whether your stories were about fabulous beings or about your next-door neighbours mattered little. In places cut off by geography or politics from the main stream of material progress this attitude persisted longer, in some cases even into our own times. The overpowering nearness and strength of the natural forces made it easy to believe in the supernatural. Indeed in wilder parts of Britain today, especially in winter, it is difficult not to believe in it, just as it is hard for an atheist to maintain his convictions on a long sea voyage. It would not be easy to prove that the much-advertised 'Celtic imagination' has anything to do with race. A people that once occupied most of Western Europe must have left much of itself in regions from which its distinctive language and customs have long since vanished. It seems better to think that the wild, remote western fringe of Europe, where alone the Celtic languages have been able to survive, provided an ideal milieu for the preservation and intensification of imaginative powers that were once the common heritage of all mankind.

The last fifty years have brought immense changes to the Highlands. Island life as described by Miss Goodrich Freer in 1902 has far more in common with the seventeenth century than with the present day. The end is not yet, and no one would be rash enough to make prophecies. The march of civilisation, which has long since robbed the English countryside of most of its individual charm, may in this wilder land remain chiefly material, providing wireless and asbestos tiles and rexine armchairs without changing the hearts of the people who use them. Or it may go further: the price demanded in exchange for our comforts and conveniences is grievously high. Before modern transport broke down the isolation of the Highlands, the life and outlook of the people remained largely Homeric. Apart from religion, their husbandry, handicrafts, and culture, as revealed in songs and stories, might have come straight out of the *Odyssey*, just as the elegies and panegyrics of the bards are oddly reminiscent of Pindar. The ease and rapidity with which the highly intelligent and adaptable Gael has assimilated an alien culture may blind us to the primitive virtues, old and true as the hills and the sea, that lie so close beneath the surface. This in part explains the immense hold of the Bible on the hearts of the Highland people. Now I had not read the Bible since girlhood until the day I bought a Gaelic version to teach myself the language: and in both Testaments alike I kept hearing the voices not of Israelites or Galileans, but of our own crofters and fishermen.

Now as is well known, the Presbyterian ministers, not having learned to tolerate, and even to assimilate harmless pagan practices, as was done by the Catholic Church at large, and more especially by St Columba and his successors, busied themselves in stamping out the old customs and traditional story-telling. Bishop Carsewell's diatribe against 'the vain, hurtful, lying worldly tales' about Fionn and his heroes set an example which has been zealously followed by men who never realised that many of the Old Testament stories belong to the same class.* Frowned upon by authority, the art of singing and story-telling was driven underground, where it survived in ever lessening power, except in the Catholic islands, where Campbell, Carmichael, and Mrs Kennedy Fraser gathered the greater part of their material. The spread of secular education did much to hasten this process. The old tales were for the most part orally transmitted, and their survival depended on long and accurate memories, which are weakened if not actually destroyed by reading. It is a sad fact, to be pondered on by educationalists, that the more we read the less we remember. 'I can look that up again,' we say, replacing the volume, and promptly forget.

The taste for story-telling, old as man's life on earth, and likely to last as long, is now partly satisfied by newspapers, magazines, and wireless, and partly by gossip, which gives

* Carsewell translated Knox's Liturgy into Gaelic in 1567.

the more personal touch. Gossip, however highly coloured, is not necessarily malicious: we do not want to miscall our neighbours, but we do want a good story. Wickedness, especially if hidden or in high places, is always more interesting than virtue – a stumbling-block to the moralist, who is forced to enliven the duller part of his message with sudden conversions and death-bed repentances. If, as in most law-abiding communities, no real wickedness is available, strangers must serve our turn. In a herd of white sheep, the doings of the black one will be the most entertaining and fruitful. When we feel inclined, as well we may, to be indignant – for few things have caused more undeserved suffering than idle gossip – we might remember that the man talked about is doing a social service. Whether he likes it or not, he has stepped into the shoes of Fionn MacCumhail, and himself become the subject of those 'vain, hurtful, lying worldly stories' that tickled the ears of our ancestors. His eccentricities have taken the place of the queer doings of fairies, monsters, and apparitions of the night. The old Gaelic laws of hospitality laid as much stress on entertainment for the mind as on food and drink for the body, and where material comforts were scarce, the need for such entertainment was all the greater. In return for what he might receive, the guest was expected to produce stories and songs, much as he is now asked for news or interesting talk. To be dissected for the entertainment of your neighbours, even without your knowledge, is only a degree less unpleasant than being stared at, though the Highlander has always the courtesy to do his staring discreetly from behind some cover. But the stranger who comes to live or stay must remember that the provision of fresh, even if involuntary amusement to his hosts is one of the few ways of repaying the kindness and hospitality he invariably receives.

The man with a literal mind may have his place in business or in the laboratory, but he is a poor companion at the fireside. It is like being forever in the witness-box. Everything you say, if not actually used against you, will be taken at its face value. The picturesque exaggeration, the ironical twist, the half-expressed allusion will be taken literally, and thus be made to stink of falsehood, and wilful falsehood at that. Such company is specially difficult for a writer who writes, not to instruct but to entertain, and mostly for his own pleasure, or for the poet concerned only with imaginative truth. For he will be apt to see more in a thing than is ostensibly there. It may be that reality is like an onion, of which the yea-yea man sees only the outermost and least attractive layer, and that there are degrees of vision corresponding with the inner rings, which certain people may have and others not; and for these last, the world beneath the skin and its apprehension may seem vanity and romance, if not deliberate falsehood.

I once had a colonial working on the farm – an intelligent middle-aged man who had had many interesting experiences abroad, and wished to write about them. During his stay we had been shifting cattle on horseback, not always without incident, though of a trivial sort. One day, to amuse my tired harvesters at dinner, I gave a graphic description of a recent round-up. My friend, knowing the cattle, my pony, and myself, accused me of deliberately touching up the tale. I protested that I was not giving evidence in a police court, and people were welcome to take the story with as many grains of salt as they wished. But in vain: he would not admit the distinction. A few weeks later, I asked him about his plans for writing. He looked grave. 'I shall never write anything now,' he declared. 'If writing involves all that sort of thing, I've no use for it.'

This made me feel rather sad. We read a book that appeals to us, and long to meet the author. Luckily we do not always get the chance. For in our passion for consistency, we want the whole man to square with his book, and if, as not seldom, he does not, we are bitterly disappointed. Often in books that are frankly autobiographical, the writer, even when stressing his faults and mistakes, presents himself in too sympathetic a light. This bias is hard to avoid, for he is instinctively obeying the law of self-preservation, and his readers see him not as he is, but as he wishes to appear. He cannot help idealising himself a little – otherwise he would hardly be human. And in this connection, is it not an awful thought that those autobiographers who leave an unpleasant picture of themselves – and many do – must be pretty bad in real life?

There is another point about writers as about artists in general. The man is his work, and anything outside it – his physical and social life, his toothache and his tempers – are irrelevant. By his work he must be judged, and by it alone. If this is true, it is surely better not to meet him, for his physical and social shortcomings may influence our judgment of his work. And if we do meet him, it must be in simple kindness, as one human being meets another, with everything else forgotten. His value to the world is his work, and it only. But his value to us as a friend comes with the discovery and appreciation of those broad human qualities he shares with all mankind.

In most places the limits of land and water are sharply defined. But in this as in much else, there is something anarchic about the West. With all its islands and promontories, its lochs of salt and fresh water, its sounds and rivers, sea fords and skerries, forever wet with rain or spray or dew, the elements are so closely intermingled that we cannot always distinguish their bounds. So also in our contemplation, the natural beauty of hill and sea, which first arouses and then intensifies our own spiritual awareness, becomes so deeply blended with it that in the end we scarcely know what comes from without and what from within. It would all be the same, we say, if no one were there to see. But would it, in every sense? For there is something in a fair landscape, as in a fair face, that shines with a borrowed light. If all conscious spirits were gone, the loveliest thing on earth would be cold and dead as the other side of the moon.

The indefinable quality of romance, which gives meaning and value to the dullest thing it touches, is with us always and everywhere, like stars in daylight, if only we choose to look. Yet there are certain people who unconsciously gather romance about them – people to whom 'things happen', people who have the power of finding a special significance in their most trivial experiences. And in the same way there are certain places where not only are deeds done that stir the imagination of men for centuries, but even the common round of work and sleep are touched with light. This quality is most often found in small islands, and also in places enisled in their own remoteness, like the country between Loch Shiel and Loch Nevis, the lonely and beautiful land of Moidart. The railway, built for the traffic of fish from Mallaig, has never brought it nearer to a world on which, in poverty or pride, it long since turned its back, nor sullied the bays of gleaming sand, and rocky capes flung out to face the peaks of Rhum, and the long faint line of the Western Isles. The scattered people, lost in deep glens and on empty shores, are all Gaelic speakers and mostly Catholic. Even the most superficial traveller gets the impression of a land pre-occupied with the pieties and fidelities of the past, with the last light of a long and glorious tradition: a land where one could cherish the forlornest hope, the most impossible loyalty, without feeling a fool.

It was in March 1940 – in days that now seem as remote as the world before Culloden – that I decided to go from Stromeferry on a visit to a friend with a sheep farm in Morvern. I wanted to follow the west coast all the way – a thing less easy than it sounds, for the glens with their sundering rivers and sea lochs run east and west, so that communications north and south are few and difficult. I travelled by steamer from Kyle to Mallaig, thence by train to Lochailort, and from there on foot through Moidart, spending a night at Glenuig, and crossing Loch Sunart by rowing-boat from Camusinas to Glencripesdale.

Lochailort is the third station out of Mallaig, and I was nearly carried past it, being absorbed in conversation with a Banffshire fisherman who knew an ex-trawler hand we had once employed on the farm. He took a gloomy view of the weather, and sure enough by the time we reached Morar a fine rain had set in. Only one other person came out of the train – a pale-faced youth with a rucksack. It was not the season for hikers, and yet he did not look like a native home on holiday. I felt sure he was also bound for Glenuig, and having no special desire for a companion on this ten-mile tramp, I went into the inn and ordered tea. The place was dismantled for spring cleaning, and I had my meal at the corner of a billiard table in the company of a talkative parrot.

By this time it was raining steadily. Highland rain is soft, harmless, and often pleasant to walk in, but now I cursed it for blotting out the unknown shapes of splendid hills. The path to Glenuig rose gradually from sea level, winding high above Lochailort. It was very rough, and here and there I saw the tracks of the postman's pony, which had passed not long before me. Two stags, apart from the rest of the herd, which was grazing above, broke down the slope in front of me: otherwise I saw no living creature. Walking in a water-proof is hot work, and, stopping to remove a sweater, I heard the crunch of footsteps. I hoped it was a shepherd with whom I might have a crack about local people and things, but it proved to be the pale young man with the rucksack. Bound for the same place, in that empty land in the rain, we could hardly avoid joining forces. I mildly suggested that if he were in a hurry he had better leave me behind, as I was a slow walker: but the device did not work. As we plodded along he told me that he came from Glasgow and was looking for a croft. No, he had little or no experience, but hoped to manage somehow. How persistent is this illusion, that an inexperienced stranger can make a living on a small croft, which will not even support the man of the country, with his knowledge and simpler standard of living! To live on a croft, you must have a little money of your own, or else some paid part-time employment; for the sale of a dozen lambs and a couple of calves will not go far towards living expenses.

At Roshven the path dropped to sea-level and widened to a carriage road, which led through the derelict policies of a shuttered mansion house. There was no approach by land except the bridle-path by which we had come, but the seaward view was magnificent, and the clouds lifted to let us see it. Beyond Roshven the road dwindled once more to a track, in places incredibly rough, which twisted and turned as it followed the rocky coast, overhung with ancient gnarled birches, and strewn with dead leaves and rotten twigs. The improvement of this path has been under discussion for thirty years, but before the first blow of a pick is heard, I think the people of Glenuig will have gone on a longer road.

The sun had vanished, leaving a quiet and clouded sky, when we rounded the last bend and came in sight of the bay of Glenuig, with a heavy motor boat riding at anchor, and several dinghies drawn up on the shingle. From the shore the narrow glen wound up into the hills, narrowing as it went, and rising to the pass that leads to Kinlochmoidart. Dotted on the braes and near the shore were a few houses, mostly one-storeyed, with little strips of land all dug by hand. Except for the mail pony, there is no horse in Glenuig: the crofts are little more than gardens, for most people keep only one cow. Near the bridge, a new telephone box leapt out at me in startling redness. It is a great boon to the people, for the nearest doctor is at Arisaig, sixteen miles away by bridle-path or boat. On a knoll to the south, sheltered by dripping trees, was a plain grey church with a small belfry, where Mass is said once in three weeks by the priest from Mingarry. There is a quietness, an austerity about Gaelic Catholicism, whether in the Highlands or in the west of Ireland, which is more easily perceived than explained. It may have come from the pressure of dominant Calvinism, or from the poverty of the people, or by the impact of wild bleak scenery on spirits naturally receptive; but whatever the cause, the fact remains. Even in Barra, an island almost entirely Catholic, there is no trace of the cliff shrines and Calvaries of Brittany. The Catholic Church in Scotland, which survived the Reformation as a handful of men on the run, mainly in the remoter Highlands and Islands, came through a grim persecution, and now, like a battered ship in port, still seems to bear the marks of that struggle.

My friend from Morvern had travelled this road before me, and had arranged for me to stay with a certain Angus Macdonald. When I asked for his house, I was surprised to be directed to Samalaman, which is some distance beyond Glenuig on the way to Smearisary. The people of the house seemed to know all about my predecessor, which was not surprising, since few strangers pass in winter, or indeed at any time, and this boy wore the kilt and spoke fluent Gaelic. But they had received no letter about me, and were much distressed that they had no bed, as the two-roomed cottage was full. Old Angus insisted on escorting me back to Glenuig, where he would help me find quarters. On the road we talked about many things, and I was struck not merely by the courtesy which is found everywhere in the remoter places and among older people, but with his high standard of education and power of expression in English, which yet remained a foreign language to him. He pointed out a half-tide rock in the bay on which, in the old penal days, a priest had been left to drown. He spoke also of a cave in which secret Masses had once been said. 'We are all Catholics here by tradition', he added, 'and Jacobite in sympathy.' His son was in the regular army, and the old man was trying to get a month's leave for him to help with the peats. The last war stripped Glenuig of its young men, and the present conflict will do the same for their sons. Yet I had the odd impression that Culloden would always mean more to them than Mons or Dunkirk.

On the road we met a man in a bonnet, carrying a milking-pail – an educated man who had taken two or three derelict crofts. He may have had his troubles, for it is difficult in war-time for strangers to settle in remote places on the coast without being thought spies. The more innocent your inter-est in birds or in scenery, the more sinister your supposed intentions. An ardent Nationalist, too, is sometimes viewed with suspicion, for, like certain Irish Republicans, he may believe that anything is better than Britain. Which may or may not be true; but the extremists must remember that the Highlanders' natural loyalty has now been transferred to the British Crown, and that as long as the Navy is full of Hebrideans and the Army retains its Highland regiments, so long will their point of view find little favour. The Axis Powers have promised an independent Celtic Confederation. The trouble is that Highlanders have no love for their fellow Gaels of Ireland, and would feel little if any more kinship with their distant cousins in Brittany and Cornwall than with the mainly Germanic people in East Anglia. 'Best as you are, my dear,' as an old Cornishwoman remarked to one contemplating marriage, 'best as you are.' A.E. said that the empire of the Celt is in Tir nan Og. By this he does not mean to banish his people to the realm of unprofitable dreams; their function, like that of both Greeks and Jews before them, may well be the spiritual penetration and leavening of their conquerors.

From the brae above the river, the old man showed me the house of another Angus Macdonald. It was the last cottage up the glen, on the way to Kinlochmoidart, low and neatly thatched. Everything about the place was tidy: there was a new byre, with a holly tree beside it, and nearby a round stack of hay which had been consumed by pulling from under the top what was required each day, till now, at the tail of winter, it looked like an enormous mushroom. The sound of footsteps brought out Angus, a spare grey-haired man in a fisherman's jersey, who had served on yachts. I was expected, and drawn into the kitchen, where he presented me to his gentle sweet-voiced wife. Their collie was cuffed away into a corner, and my own dog installed at the fire. Presently the wireless was turned on, but nothing came out but a few uncertain sounds. For a while Angus tinkered at it without effect. 'That thing is almost dead,' I remarked in Gaelic. 'It is indeed,' he replied. 'I prefer the paper myself.' 'So do I,' I agreed, and we switched it off. There were only two rooms in the house, and the one in which I slept was half parlour, half bedroom. There was a peat fire burning for me, and – strange anomaly in this timeless place – four clocks all going at once, and ticking very loud and out of time. At my request, three of them were removed.

That night, being healthily tired, I went to bed early, but it was long before I slept. From the next room came the murmur of talk in Gaelic; then they recited the Rosary together, and at last when sleep took them, I heard nothing but the tinkle of a burn and the brush of wind against the little panes. The dog was dreaming at the embers, and out in the byre their cow lay warmly bedded in bracken. It seemed to me then, as before in the house of an old shepherd I knew, that the crown of marriage, as a lifelong companionship, comes when old people sit together at the fire, and walk down hand in hand into the shadows. I thought of this, and afterwards had a strange feeling that I, a stranger, had been in this place before; that this language, which I understood only as a foreigner, had not been learned but recalled. It was as if, after some immense and uncharted voyage, I had at last come into port. Such intimations, though not uncommon, are hard to explain: but in no other place have I been made to feel that the past exists in and beside the present, and at times can break in upon our daily life and for the moment suspend it. Geographical remoteness, the old religion, the intense Highland sense of tradition, must all have combined to produce this effect, and it was overwhelming.

I have spoken of the deep interest still taken in the events of 1745. Now one of the oddest things about the '45 is that its celebrity is out of all proportion to its historical importance. It certainly ended a social epoch, but this would have come anyhow, for the growing power and influence of the prosperous South was already making itself felt in the Highlands, attracting and moulding the impressionable Celt. But there were two forces: the personal charm of the Prince, which gave him an unmerited hold on the hearts of men, and the Highland genius for faithfulness – a quality seen not so much in the gentry, whose temptations to disloyalty were greater, but in the common people, content to give life and money to lairds who not seldom betrayed them. Fidelity – that great virtue of seamen – is also developed by the hard life of mountain people: hills and sea make men, and work them to a fine edge. Moidart was decimated in the last war, and now may well lose the next generation of its manhood. The survivors live on in the mute uncomplaining patience with which Highland people have too often accepted their fate, allowing, in indolence or irony, the city Nationalist to plead their cause, already for this reason lost.

The dawn brought heavy showers, with the promise of more rain later. Before starting on my fifteen-mile walk to Salen, I looked hopefully round the house, and not finding what I sought, asked discreetly in Gaelic: 'Where is the little house?' 'Mo *chreach!*' my hostess exclaimed in great distress, for she had been in service with a nobleman, 'there is no little house in it at all!' 'It is all the same,' I replied cheerfully. 'Better with me is the wood!'

The path from Glenuig to Kinlochmoidart rose steeply over a pass from the head of the glen, from which, looking back, you get a view extending from the Cuillins in the north-west to the hills of Mull in the south-west, with Eigg and Rhum in the foreground and the Outer Islands like a cloud-bank beyond. But that day the clouds hung low, and I did not see anything but the little houses of Glenuig and the grey waters of the bay. The flat stretch at the top of the pass was dotted with numerous cairns, marking the places where coffins were set down on the long journey to the burial ground at Mingarry.

That night I slept at the inn of Salen on Loch Sunart, and next morning walked down the lochside to Camusinas, where a boat was to come for me from Glencripesdale on the Morvern side. Arriving before the appointed time, I stayed talking and drinking tea in a croft house nearby. The woman of the house hung a large towel on a fence at the foreshore, in the hope that the housekeeper at Glencripesdale Lodge would take it as a signal and warn the boatman. She must have done so, for a boat soon appeared, manned by a wild, ragged-looking fellow with a pleasant smile and an outboard engine that ran as smoothly as if we had been on the Thames. All payment was refused, and a young shepherd insisted on guiding me across the hill, until my friend's farm was in sight. But I had left my heart in Glenuig, and resolved to spend two nights there on my way home.

The day came for my return, and with it the bad weather. Rain had begun to fall when we left the house, and by the time we reached the top of the pass, from which Loch Sunart was visible, the wind, luckily at our backs, had risen to gale force. The narrow winding loch was lashed to white, and I realised there was little hope of crossing that day, unless the wind should fall at sunset. Glencripesdale Lodge was officially closed, but the housekeeper, who was there alone with one of the maids, invited us in to have tea and wait for an improvement. By six o'clock the case was obviously hopeless, and I was asked to spend the night at the Lodge. Storm-stayed, as Dr Johnson might have been – for Glencripesdale can be reached only by boat or on horseback – I was glad to accept the offer, and spent the night among the eerily echoing corridors of the great empty Victorian mansion, with its tower and pitch-pine woodwork and vast slatted larder and Blackface rams grazing beneath the dining-room window. Tomorrow, I thought, I shall sleep in the two-roomed thatched house at Glenuig. All night it rained and blew, but the dawn came without wind or cloud – one of those Highland 'pet days' for which one would willingly endure a month of gale and deluge. The loch was like glass and the boat waiting. We sped across in time for me to catch the Ardnamurchan mail-bus which would take me as far as Acharacle on the way back to Glenuig. I dawdled along the now familiar road, but seeing new sights, because of the transient brilliance and clearness of that day of truce. For truce it was, and no more. When I reached Glenuig and went down to the shore to look at the western sea, faint wisps of cirrus were fanning out from behind Rhum; the points of the coast were in startling relief, and the far horizon was dim and spongy.

Next day in drenching showers, I visited the little township of Smearisary, which lies on a wild promontory jutting far into the sea, and approached by a rough boggy track unfit for wheels. Here in scattered pockets and flats among rocks are the dwindling remains of a crofting community. Most of the people are gone, and the houses in ruins. Only four households remain, and the people are all beyond middle age. The life is hard, for there is no pony in the place, and all tillage must be done by hand, and all transport with creels. Nor is the exposed coast friendly to boats. I visited the peat-moss, which lies secluded at the bottom of a deep narrow gully. It is approached by the roughest of paths, sometimes lost in water, along which all the fuel of Smearisary must be carried in creels. In a soft place I saw a footprint, small and pointed, made by one of those shiny, insubstantial rubber boots beloved of women. So it was a woman who carried those creels of hard-won peats. The sight saddened me. It was the old story – the failure of manpower, the beginning of the end.

I had a message to one of the houses, where lived a woman who had once been in service in Morvern. I was asked into a spotless kitchen, half-filled by two large beds with white curtains and covers. The man of the house spoke halting English, and had the wild shy air of one who hardly ever meets a stranger. On leaving, I was seen part of the way home, according to the hospitable Highland custom. When my escort left me, I stood for a minute on the crest, and looked down on the houses nestling in the shelter of great rocks, with windows looking steadfastly from under the thatch at the plains of the sea and the vast dome of the sky, and upon the tiny strips of green pasture, with cattle grazing at peace. How fair it would seem in the long twilight of June, how fair it seemed even now in the cold wild squalls of March. But when these people go, the place will be desolate, for there will be no man left to dig the land and haul the boats.

I expected to walk back to Lochailort station by the way I had come. But Angus told me that the big boat would be going for stores in the morning, and if I arranged overnight, they would start earlier, so that I could catch the Mallaig train. He promised to look at the weather at sunrise, and if it seemed threatening, would call me early enough to walk, in case the boat should not go.

The morning was reasonably fair, and I was down at the shore before nine. Two boys were ready with a dinghy, and in silence we pulled out to the big motor boat – a solid roomy craft, broad in the beam, high in the gunwale, built for the western seas in winter. She was heavily tarred outside, but without one lick of paint on any part not technically in contact with salt water. The engine started without too much trouble. There was a moment off Roshven when it faded out with a sigh, and we wallowed aimlessly in the long swell, and the boys exchanged vague and embarrassed glances, but apart from this we had little to complain of. The lads, with the fresh faces and greenish-grey eyes of the country, said not one word to me or to each other, except for polite monosyllabic replies to remarks of mine which died on the air, as if scared of the vastness above and beneath. Yet on the sea there is no embarrassment in silence, for wind and waves make their own conversation, and the knowledge of your boat's frailty acts as a bridle on the tongue.

All the way up Lochailort we were stopping at this rock and that, picking up wet, heavy bags of winkles left on some handy ledge for collection. After a number of these halts I began to get worried about my train, for I saw ahead, on an islet, what looked like a whole array of other bags. But on closer view it proved to be basking seals, and we chugged on without stopping. The train, detained for the inspection of permits, was not yet in, and the stationmaster was having a telephone conversation in Gaelic with his colleague at Arisaig. When he had done, I mentioned the winkles. 'Yes,' he replied, 'they all go to London. It is a strange thing how fond the English are of shellfish. Now we don't think much of them ourselves.'

The island group of the Blaskets, at the extreme end of the mountainous peninsula of Corcaguiney in Kerry, contains the most westerly inhabited land in Europe, and the last lighthouse to be seen by emigrants on their way to the New World. Only one of the group, the Great Blasket, a high narrow island three miles long and one mile wide, is now inhabited. It is not more than three and a half miles from the mainland, but the crossing must be made in canvas canoes, and the heavy Atlantic swell often prevents landing. The village is on the eastern side above the little harbour, and holds a population of about 156, who live on the produce of their crofts, on lobster and mackerel fishing, and of recent years on the teaching of Irish. There is plenty of peat on the island, and asses to carry it; but there are no horses, and no boats but the long narrow canoes, made of tarred canvas stretched on a wooden framework, which are handled by the men with superb seamanship. There is a school but no shops, and no church except on the mainland, where Mass is heard by the islanders whenever the weather is fit.

The people seem to have come to the island in the hungry days of the eighteenth and early nineteenth centuries, when hosts of evicted peasants were seeking refuge on the coast. They have led the hard precarious lives of most small islanders, with bursts of prosperity in good times, but too often verging on starvation when harvests failed on land and sea. It is a life that breeds courage and resource, a stoic fatalism, and a not unnatural carelessness about the morrow. At the beginning of the present century the Great Blasket was taken over by the Congested Districts Board; the people were protected from excessive rents, and their houses rebuilt by their own paid labour. During the last war the U-boat campaign brought much wealth to the island in the shape of drifting cargoes that could be consumed or sold. And more recently the Gaelic revival has drawn many scholars and students to study Irish, where, as in Aran, it still remains in its original purity.

These things alone might give the Blasket a unique interest. But in addition, the island has produced a literature which can speak of the old things in the old language, not with wistful or sentimental regret, but in a manner both vital and modern. Within the last twelve years this little community of crofters and fishermen has produced three published autobiographies written in Irish: *An tOileanach* (The Islandman), by Tomas O'Crohan; *Fiche Bliain ag Fas* (Twenty Years A-growing), by Maurice O'Sullivan; and *Peig*, by Peg Sayers. All gained an immediate success in the original, and the first two were translated into English and had a great vogue. Nor is this as surprising as it may seem at first sight. Schooling in the Blasket was often intermittent, but the people, like many other Munster peasants, had always a wealth of folk songs and tales. In the social disintegration of the eighteenth century, poets and scholars were scattered among the people, and much of their work was transmitted orally or copied in manuscripts that lay hidden under the thatch of many a cabin.

Tomas O'Crohan was born in 1856, and his book was published in Irish in 1929 and translated in 1934. He was encouraged to write it by Mr Brian O'Kelly, who read him part of Gorki's autobiography to show him the interest of such work. He gives his own reason for writing, and we can surely find no better: 'To set down the character of the people about me, so that some record might live after us, for the like of us will never be seen again.' The book is written in a simple objective way, but it abounds in fine episodes of fishing, seal-hunting, and merry-making on the mainland, with many a shrewd observation of life and character. The man himself stands out as a keen but kindly observer, capable, versatile, enjoying his good times with light-hearted gaiety, and meeting adversity with the islander's habitual fortitude. Two of his children were taken by illness and two by the sea. Of the last, who was drowned in an attempt to save the daughter of a visitor, he says: 'I hope that they (*i.e.* the girl's parents) didn't think I was angry with them, because my son died for their daughter. I was never so foolish as that. If it was for her he died, it could not be helped. It was God's will.' He has a keen interest in his native tongue for its own sake, and also because he realises that the pure Irish of the Blasket is of great value to scholars. 'I hear many an idle fellow saying that there is no use in our native tongue. But that has not been my experience. Only for it I should have been begging my bread.'

Maurice O'Sullivan is still a comparatively young man. His autobiography, which was written to entertain his friends in the Blasket, was translated in 1933, and became something of a bestseller. He opens with a sentence which gives a complete and beautiful picture of his setting: 'I am a boy who was born and bred in the Great Blasket, a small truly Gaelic island which lies north-west of the coast of Kerry, where the storms of the sky and the wild sea beat without ceasing from end to end of the year, and from generation to generation against the wrinkled rocks which stand above the waves that wash in and out of the coves where the seals have their homes.' The first part of the book contains vivid descriptions of island life, of fishing and hunting, of dances and ceilidhs, of neighbours and of visitors in search of Irish. In the second part he tells how he left the Blasket to become a Civic Guard in Connemara. The book, which is written in rather a lighter vein than O'Crohan's, is brimming over with vitality and high spirits. There are passages of vivid description; the author has a real gift for telling a tale, and the language is full of raciness and beauty.

The third autobiography was written some years ago by Peg Sayers, an old woman of the island. As far as I know it has not yet been translated, and the only Irish copy I ever saw was on a bookshelf in Barra, before I knew a word of the language.

I cannot help thinking that, in spite of Government grants and propaganda, spoken Irish has less vitality than Scottish Gaelic. Even in 1905 the Norwegian scholar Marstrander was complaining that the Irish of the Kerry mainland was too much mixed with English to be of value to him. At about the same time the child O'Sullivan, whose mother died at his birth, was sent to be brought up in Dingle, a town whose position in Kerry corresponds to that of Oban in Argyll. Here he managed to reach school age not only without hearing a word of Irish, but even without knowing that such a tongue existed. Two years ago, when walking in the remote parts of West Kerry, which is a recognised part of the Gaeltacht or Irish-speaking district, I never heard a word of Irish used to man or beast – a thing unthinkable in Morvern or Coigeach.

But if we have more Gaelic in Scotland, we have as yet no O'Crohans or O'Sullivans. One wonders why. Perhaps it is not without significance that the first printed book in Gaelic was Bishop Carsewell's translation of Knox's Liturgy. Since the Reformation Gaelic has been too much chained to the pulpit, as, on the other side, it has been bound up with a backward-looking patriotism whose world ended at Culloden. Today, the production of songs for Mods and concerts is the chief activity of Gaelic writers; and the fitting of new words to traditional tunes has yielded too large a crop of melodious but hackneyed verse, which is popular, as Moore's *Irish Melodies* was popular, but hardly does justice to the beautiful language in which it is written.

Many causes are at work, and not least the strange demands of the British public, and the courtesy, half indolent, half ironical, with which the Highlander yields to them. Clearances and proscriptions are no more, but patronage and gushing sentimentality may prove a subtler danger. No country has been more written about or more slobbered over than the Hebrides. People converge from both sides of the Atlantic, seeking for romance to lighten the drabness of civilisation, or for mystery as a cure for materialism. There seems to be a ceaseless demand for books and articles written to a familiar recipe – a few seabirds, a handful of wild flowers, the sun setting in the western ocean, a legend or two, an anecdote of the '45, and a few tags of Gaelic. The people do not speak for themselves; they sit and let themselves be written about by outsiders or *émigrés* catering for the world-weariness of the townsman. Thus the objective simplicity of the genuine folk-songs, which is also found in the earlier Irish and Scottish Gaelic literature, is overlaid with spurious romance. This can be studied by anyone who takes up a volume of *Songs of the Hebrides* and troubles to compare the Gaelic with the English versions, where the direct and often plain language of the original is touched up to meet the concert-goer's demand for wistful sentimentality.

Now the inevitable reaction has set in, and in some quarters it is fashionable to 'debunk' the Highlands, as Mr MacNeice has done in his book *I Crossed the Minch*. But to substitute discussions and anecdotes for seal-croons and sea-sorrows will get us no further. The Highlands and Islands are full of men and women of character and intelligence who have lived a fine full life on land and sea. If some of these could be persuaded to write about themselves and their days as they really were, and to write (or dictate) in Gaelic, we should have something to put beside the Blasket books; and there would be no lack of translators to introduce our Highland authors to a wider public. What has been done in the 'small truly Gaelic island' of 150 people, might surely be done in the hundreds of square miles of the western Highlands and Islands.

It was at midnight, and in winter, that I first set eyes on the isle of Barra. We crossed the Minch in storm and driving rain; but soon after leaving Lochboisdale the wind died away, and we made our landfall under clearing skies and on a sea whose black and polished surface reflected the harbour beacons. The *Lochearn* stole past the shadow of Muldoanich, wallowing in the long swell that rolled in from the Atlantic through the narrows of Vatersay. Save for a glimmer from the canvas-screened bridge, the upper deck was in darkness: the mast-head lamp swung in a wide slow arc among the stars. Ahead, under the lowering mass of Heaval, were the clustered lights of Castlebay, with its houses and curing sheds, and high on the rock the church of Our Lady, Star of the Sea. As we drew alongside the pier, the sheen from the lamps fell on a host of upturned faces, eager, expectant, for no one goes to bed without seeing the boat come in. I went ashore under the wing of one of those commercial travellers of the isles who ply their trade precariously in rowing-boats and in pony-traps, and can tell, over a cup of strong stewed tea, tales that have a faint but authentic flavour of the Arabian Nights. Next day, in return for his kindness, I went to the village hall and helped him to arrange a show of Glasgow boots and shoes, not one of which was suited to the rocks and bogs of the Western Isles.

It was later on a Sunday afternoon that I discovered the fittest if not the most beautiful burial ground in the world. It was one of those wild, brilliant north-westerly days that follow a great gale. A stiff breeze was still blowing, with an occasional rattle of hail from hard-edged anvil-headed clouds. Between showers the February sun was warm, and I scrambled along the rocky southern fringe of Halaman Bay in a vain attempt to photograph the immense breakers that were rolling in upon the sands. When I had gone far enough to see round and over the northern horn of the bay, I caught sight of a further promontory flung far into the ocean, and at its extremity a walled enclosure full of headstones and crosses. It was more than a mile away in a direct line, and separated by an expanse of heaving green water, laced and marbled with foam, over which the shining crests of waves chased one another shoreward, and the noise that went up drowned every other sound. Turning back, I skirted Bachd and crossed the mouth of the glen that holds the crofting townships of Borve and Craigston. Here I left the road and walked across the short turf towards the burial ground. The point on which it stood was low, and fringed with shelving rock, and the brilliant green grass came to the level of the high spring tides. There were some Barra ponies grazing near, dun, strongly built, with flowing manes and tails, and a few cross-bred sheep, some with lambs, for spring comes early to the sea pastures. The Ordnance Survey marks the site of a chapel of St Brendan the Navigator, but at that time

I could find no trace of the ruins. They lie close above a little cove on the southern side, where the coracles beloved of Irish saints could have found a landing.

The sagging gate, secured with a bit of string, left plenty of room for the traffic of sheep, and I was not surprised to find a ewe inside, resting under the lee of the wall, and her lamb playing among the graves. And who would put them out, for these walls are the only shelter on the whole wind-swept promontory, and the grass within is rich and sweet. The gravestones, old and new alike, were weathered to one grey, tufted with lichen, encrusted with salt, as if coeval with the rocks on which they stood. The sun, shooting out from a retreating hail-cloud, lay warmly on the place, and I sat down for a while beside the ewe, who did not trouble to move. At the little church on the edge of the sands, people were coming out from Benediction, the older ones in their Sunday blacks, the younger in clothes more modern. But these distant figures, dispersing up the glen or along the shore, soon dwindled or vanished; and all sounds of man or beast were swallowed up in the vast annihilating roar of the sea.

I looked over the parapet of the west wall, with the salty tang of spray on my lips, and saw nothing but tumbling green water, and a smother of snow-white foam, and shining clouds piled on the sharp horizon. Fifty miles out, at that low level invisible, was the lonely Isle of St Kilda, in Gaelic called Hirt, which is said to be an ancient word for death, and beyond that the empty wastes of ocean. Later, I thought, the sun will go down in cloud-banks and trailing showers, and this burial-ground, with its freight of memories and prayers, will slowly sink into darkness and the dead be left alone with the sea, now and for ever. A race of seamen, who in merchantmen and trawlers, in smacks and battleships, have given so many lives to the deep, might want to be buried in some sheltered glen where the noise of the surf is no more than a murmur, or at least in a place that faces the quieter waters of the Minch, and the sun rising over the kindly hills of the mainland. But no: for not only in Barra, but in other western isles, the dead are buried on the edge of wild ocean, as if there were some special grace in the nearness of the sea that was at once their field of labour, their grave, and their symbol of eternity. Alexander Carmichael speaks of a crofter in Uist who every morning went out to look at the sea, and baring his head, exclaimed, '*Nach urramach an cuan!*' (How worthy of reverence is the ocean). And it seemed to me then that over that broken gate, with its traffic of ewes and lambs, might be inscribed those imperishable words, *Hic est requies mea in aeternum.*

One Sunday evening in March, I found myself on the road to Kyle. The Mallaig boat leaves early on Monday morning, and those without car or cycle must walk overnight, for there is no suitable train. Heavy rain had fallen, and in the shelter of the Duncraig woods the air was moist and stagnant. Faint wispy clouds lay crosswise in layers over the sky, like cobwebs among rafters, and a blurred, milky half-moon was reflected in many a puddle. At the foot of the long ascent to Loch Lundie, where the road was still covered with stones and coarse gravel washed down long ago by a flood, I threw off my rucksack and took a rest. Once clear of the trees at the summit, I should meet the cool air that draws across the water from Skye, tempering the heat of the closest day in summer.

After a while I continued my journey. The loch lay wide and unruffled, guarded on the south by steep rocky escarpments, and on the west by pine woods in which a wandering breeze was softly moaning. Night had already invaded the rushy derelict pastures, reducing their hillocks and hollows to a uniform featureless grey. But the loch, like all calm waters, from a moss pool to the plains of ocean, had robbed the sky of its last light, and lay like a burnished shield without shadow or blemish. From its northern shore extended a long narrow spit planted with pines; and the water behind it, screened from the west by those thick dark trees, lay black and still as polished ebony. Three swans were floating there; and though in shadow, they shone with a luminous whiteness as if lit up from within.

At the western end of the loch the road was once more overshadowed with trees, and the sighing of wind through a million pine needles passed to and fro above my head as I walked. There were fences on either side, with rotten posts and broken wires round which the bracken in July grew shoulder-high. The road with its ruts and puddles, its moaning trees, was full of ghosts of the happy and forever vanished past, when Peter and I sauntered at the tail of cattle, or at the horse's head with loads of wood and fern. Then I emerged on the open fields round Achnadarroch, and found myself sniffing the raw, dead air of March for the scent of hay drying on the fences. The empty forsaken parks, overgrown with rushes like the rest, were now indistinguishable, but the last glimmer of day lingered on the white walls of the farmhouse. For a moment I stood by the burn where we used to water the cows, listening to its frail music, and watching for smoke that would never rise again for us. The Cuillins were wrapped in mist, and beyond the Sound was nothing but greyness. I turned away and continued my journey, past the oak wood which gave the farm its name, and down the brae till I reached another stretch of level road shadowed by moaning pine trees. This too was full of ghosts. On such a night, and in this very place, I had waited for our cart, long overdue from Plockton. I found myself listening for the rumble of cart-wheels, and peering through the shadows for the looming shape of the black horse, with the boy at his head. Behind me the little white house was still glimmering on the hill, faint as the sheen of broken water in starlight. I turned my back on it and went on my way, resolving never to take that road again.

Our love of idealising the past is nowhere more easily indulged than in the Highlands, where tradition is powerful enough to impress even the most superficial visitor. *Ionndrainn*, the longing for things gone beyond recall, is perhaps the most frequent, as it is the most moving note of Gaelic poetry,* and we need no 'Celtic gloom' to explain what is natural enough in a home-loving people who have long been forced by poverty and other external forces to seek a living abroad. A Highland woman – one of those who had 'forgotten' her Gaelic – told me that she did not care for Gaelic songs because they were all so sad. The best ones are, no doubt; and many a cheerful ditty is sung to the most heart-breaking air. But this is not peculiar to Gaelic. I could think of a dozen English or Lowland songs that are no whit merrier. The demand for artificial cheerfulness and self-conscious amusement, like the art of killing time, seems to

---

* Cf. A stanza by Dr. Maclachlan of Rahoy:
  'Mi air m'uilinn air an t-sliabh,
    'S mi ri iargain na bheil bhuam;
  'S tric mo shuil a' sealltuinn siar
    Far an laigh a' ghrian 's a' chuan.'
  ['On my elbow on the hill,
    I long for what is gone from me;
  Often my eye gazes westward
    Where the sun is setting in the sea.']

be a modern thing, unknown and unsought in the old world where people took things as they came. And apart from this, just as a Gregorian chant will sound dreary to ears accustomed to Victorian hymn tunes, so will the older folk-music seem strange and mournful when taken out of its setting. It is only when we go by ourselves into the wilderness, and listen to the sound of wind and running water and the song of birds, that we shall know this music for what it is – the natural and unspoilt voice of man.

I have often spoken in these essays of the uncivilised man's fatalism. Against natural powers such acquiescence is the highest wisdom. But there are other forces which we must oppose or perish. A new and horrible form of predestination has swept the world. It is the age of this or that, we say, and we must make the best of it. We cannot change anything, because we are the slaves of economic laws. Yet economic laws are the outcome of man's activity, and could not exist without his will. There was a time when a society not based on slavery was thought impossible. Now we have (at least in law) abolished slavery; and if we chose, could also abolish war and poverty and unemployment. But we do not choose; and the doctrine of Economic Law saves us the trouble of asking why not. The venerable Jewish heresy – that riches are a sign of God's favour – was given a new lease of life by the Reformers, and has followed the march of civilisation till its shadow threatens the whole world.

Regions on the outer fringe have suffered most, because the 'progress' has been too rapid to be properly assimilated; it has come like the sweep of a spring tide through a narrow channel. Within a generation, the whole outward structure of Highland, and especially island life has been transformed: how far the inward change has gone we have yet to estimate. The islanders, however poor, were once sufficient to themselves. Now they depend for all their clothing, for most of their food, and for an increasing amount of their culture, on a mainland which, for reasons of geography alone, must always remain alien. It is a melancholy fact that the changes that seem best in themselves have come too late to serve their true purpose. In the nineteenth century the cry was all for land which was not to be had. Today, when much public money has been spent on the provision of adequate crofts, they are no longer sought after, because the young people prefer the shorter hours and higher wages of industry. So also with Gaelic. The provision (in 1917) of Gaelic teaching in Highland schools came too late to arrest the decline of the spoken language. In many cases the clause was not taken advantage of, because parents had come to believe that 'there was no money in the Gaelic'. It reminds me of the tale of a farmer whose brother fell ill of pneumonia. He grudged the pay of the nurse who might have saved him, but spent four times the amount on whisky for the funeral!

By the time I reached Duirinish it was too dark to see the scars of war construction on the level croft lands. Night is kinder than we often think, not only bringing home wanderers in flesh or in remembrance, but shielding the lonely who have none to expect or evoke, from harsh lights and prying eyes. The rhythm of day and night, regular and quieting as the tides, is at the heart of Nature – 'the evening and the morning were the first day', and every other day until Doom. We grumble at the long dark nights of winter, and yet if we were given a sun that goes not down, we should soon be asking back the gift. Even the long-drawn days of midsummer in northern Scotland become wearisome after a while, and we are not sorry when August brings a few hours of real darkness. This is one reason why the life of great cities is fundamentally wrong. There we do literally turn night into day, and get no time for rest, recuperation, or meditation. In the glare of street lamps, which will return with the other blessings of peace, we are hardly aware of moon or stars, still less of the intriguing noises of the night. Only perhaps in the small hours comes a pause, when we may hear a footfall in the street, a cat on the roof, a softly purring car, and far away perhaps a passing train – the only mechanism which at night seems to have borrowed the mystery of migrating birds.

But in the country night is often too beautiful, too intriguing to let us sleep very long. Many a time in Barra have I deliberately kept awake in the softness of blankets to listen to the waves breaking below, or roused myself early in the dim winter dawn to watch the moon sinking into a grey and heaving sea.

Though we are creatures that work by day and sleep by night, there is no doubt that darkness stirs some hidden depth of personality lying dormant through the hours of communal daylight. The effect of the Polar night on human beings, as we see it in the writings of Captain Scott and Cherry Garrard and Admiral Byrd, is of unique interest: and everyone who reflects a little, and turns over a few books, even if no more than Shakespeare and the Bible, will realise that the deepest experiences of our own lives, and the most solemn moments in history and literature, have come at night.

There is only one kind of night that brings nothing but fear and oppression – the pit-murk night of fog and drizzle, when we walk sightless as if in a moving tunnel, and the light we carry does no more than throw our own shadows on the walls of vapour enclosing us. This is no true night, but the thick darkness of Egypt's plague. For the essence of night is not the loss but the heightening of vision, as if our child-ish belief were really true – that the sky is a dome, and the stars no more than holes one might prick with a pin, letting through the light of boundless space.

'Better a short sitting than a long standing' says the Gaelic proverb. I wonder what was in the mind of the old fellow who first put this dark thought into words. For it is a trouble-some, subversive saying, like 'Take no thought for the morrow', which has puzzled good Christians for nearly two thousand years. Perhaps it means 'Better one day's contemplation than seven days of action'. I once asked a boy of twenty what he was meaning to do with his life. 'I don't know yet,' was the reply. 'Money is no good in itself, but I must make enough to be able to look at things and think.' In this he showed a wisdom beyond his years, though few of us, even with full purses, are free to sit and think from one week's end to another. And perhaps it is as well: for undis-ciplined as we are, it would soon come to sitting without thinking at all. And at that stage, we might as well get up and dig the garden.

But Sunday is different. Peter Abelard, who never knew the Presbyterian sabbath, said that the life of the blessed in Paradise was one long Sunday. And even on earth good farmers, while their wives are roasting the Sunday joint, walk round their fields to contemplate the growth and work of the past week. The baser sort may also scheme for the future, but such smartness will get them no further, for a seven-day week is not only godless but inhuman. There must be one day when we can stop shouting and rushing about, and give ourselves time to listen and think, time to open our mind and senses to whatever comes from without or within, which is the best use of leisure.

On Sunday, then, when it is not pouring with rain or bitterly cold, I walk on the hill, without rod or gun or camera, just to look at things and absorb them. The first three hundred feet of the ascent are very steep, and more than once I take a spell, and sitting on the soft damp ground, look down on the strath where we live and work. It lies between hills and sea loch, with broad strips of cultivation broken by rocky knolls of birch and rowan, and in the midst the Ascaig river winds among whins and alders. From the bridge a road ascends to the brow of the pass, with maybe a cart rumbling up or a car sliding down. Here and there are houses; the older ones rise naturally from their stances, like the rocks and trees around them, while the new ones have a come-by-chance look, as if they had been dropped where they are, but certainly not from heaven. The moss holds yet a stack or two of last year's peats, and at the edge of the Laird's stubble a heap of rubbish marks the site of a rick of oats, from which the bottom sheaves were recently brought home with much squealing of rats and scampering of terriers among the legs of the patient cart-horse.

So often have I looked down upon this strath, at every season and under all skies, that my eye, being trained to expect certain shapes and outlines, is quick to spot anything unfamiliar, even if it is only a sheep's head appearing over a

far ridge, or the flash of a boy's tin pail at the well by the stepping-stones. Noises float up, clear, even loud, for the steep
hillsides act as a sounding-board, but they are detached,
disembodied, as if heard from beyond a frontier: the anxious
call of a ewe, the chink of harrows, a cock crowing, the ring of
an axe, the clump of tackety boots on a wooden footbridge.

There are many Sundays on the hill that I could recall,
but now I am thinking of one in the middle of June, when
I went up to see the flowering of the cotton-grass. I climbed
through thickets of birch with gleaming trunks and young
leaves crinkled and brilliantly green, till the path emerged
on a bare steep brae, and then dipping over a pass, fell gently
into a shallow cup in the hills, which is the entrance to the
craggy upland of the eight lochs. A burn flowing out of Loch
na Gillean wound lazily through the boggy flat, as if saving
its strength for the plunge into the gorge it had carved for
itself through rock and gravel scree. As I entered this cup,
it was as if a solid door had closed behind me. In winter or
early spring, when frost or drought has stilled the voice of
birds and running water, the silence is so deep that it can be
heard. In summer there are sounds in plenty, but wild and
lonesome ones – the croak of a raven, the drone of a passing
bee, the sighing of reeds, and the lap of water on stone.

At the near end of Loch na Gillean I found a little beach of
gravel where in hot dry weather the sheep gather to drink.
Here I sat while the warmth shed down from the sky met
the warmth that rose from the earth, and mingling, they
embraced me. Leaning back I looked into the fathomless
blue over which clouds were moving, themselves far off, but

seeming near in comparison with infinite space. There were bands and whirls and fronds of cirrus, and, below them, woolly tufts of alto-cumulus with melting edges, a sign of good weather. I tried to screen my eyes from the lower clouds, in order to see the movement of the cirrus without the confusion caused by watching things travelling at different speeds in the same field of vision. A shadow fell on my upturned face – the swift shadow of a buzzard alone in the empty sky. Then dazzled by excess of light, I rolled over on my face, and began to study the innumerable life of the ground. Ling and bell-heather mingled with sweet vernal grass and sheep's fescue and square-stemmed sedges, with here and there the small shy flowers of the hill – butterwort and bog-asphodel and potentilla, and a pale mauve orchis with dark and delicate pencillings. In places where the peaty soil, bared by recent burning, was packed hard and close, orange and grey lichens were growing, as on the surface of rock. Through these thickets, to them a portentous jungle, small spiders fought their way, and little shining beetles made daring explorations. On a low ridge above my head, gleaming against the purple of a distant hill, a dozen plumes of cotton-grass nodded and swayed in the breeze.

These silken tassels, so airy and shining, ravished me in childhood, and the passing of years has only sharpened my delight. No plant is oftener seen on Highland hills, lovely and gallant in its prime, and in death crumbling to swell the layer of more recent peat, which extends some seven feet above the old forest stratum. 'Cotton-grass', like many another English flower name, is more homely than imaginative; and to use

the botanical name *Eriophorum angustifolium* is like putting
a pack-saddle on a butterfly. In Gaelic it is called 'canach', a
word that seems connected with the Latin *canus*, meaning
white or hoary. On lower ground the cotton-grass flowers in
May and June, and on the high hills it lingers until August. In
a calm winter, plumes that have not drifted to seed remain
on the stem, draggled with rain and plastered with dead
midges, waiting with the bleached ghosts of heath-bells
for the conquering thrust of a new generation. Like other
sedges, the canach yields an early bite for sheep, and I have
often wondered if its wild silk could be spun or put to other
use. 'With the silky substance which invests the seeds,' says
Anne Pratt, 'paper and wicks of candles have been made, and
pillows stuffed.' But she does not add by whom; and I fancy
such things could only be made and used in fairy mounds.

On level tracts round lochs or beside burns, wherever
there is little drainage, even on a brae, if there are wet pockets overlying rock, the canach blooms in sheets and drifts of
white. A sunbeam sliding between clouds will set it suddenly
gleaming, a tossing sea of airy heads. But it needs the solemn
sheen of a June midnight to reveal its whole beauty in mass.
Then it lies like enchanted water under the moon, or the
floor of a corrie when stars come out at the tail of autumn
snow. The power of the Highland summer night to bring out
the essential colour in flowers, as though by some inward
illumination, is incredible until seen, and then can never be
forgotten. Many a night, on the way home from fishing, I
would see the big garden poppies glowing with something
richer than their noonday pomp of scarlet, and tapered

lupins rise motionless like candles lighted from within. Until the end of May, the field below my house is full of Cheviot ewes and their lambs. At nightfall each lamb lies, a spot of snow, to the lee of its dam; and as I pass, a score of white faces turn curiously, lighted by the gleam from the north, where, not very far away, the sun still moves above the horizon. Gulls, drawn by the freshly turned earth of a neighbouring strip of ploughland, sit on the grass in long still rows. The whiteness of lambs, of ewes' faces, of the breasts of gulls, is far beyond anything seen in the brightest noonday sun. And the first night that is light enough to reveal essential colour is a thing to wait for all the year.

Another Sunday in late July, a day of quiet skies and the lightest of breezes, I went once more to the hill. Wandering idly among drifts of cotton-grass, I gathered a few ripe heads and pulled them apart. With back to the wind I set the winged seeds free, to see how far they would go and where each one would land. For they travel incredibly far, as if there were some purpose in their wantonness, and they were propelled not by the wind but of their own free will. Most of them come to earth and are caught among heather or rushes, where they seem not prisoners but guests: but some I have seen sticking to the moist side of a freshly cut peat, and these, drying with the sod, must end upon a crofter's hearth.

A few days later I was in a rowing-boat, pulling towards the stone pier on the island of Tanera. A faint south-westerly breeze drew down the glen, hardly enough to flute the water and break the pattern of weed and stones at the bottom. On the right the hill called Meall Mor broke in steep braes to the anchorage, where it ended in a little cliff set with bushes. Suddenly, glancing over my shoulder, I saw an airy thing, bright as an insect from the Elysian fields, come floating down the glen. For a moment it hovered above the water as if to settle; and then, caught by some current of air from under the cliff, it rose quickly and vanished into the blue. For awhile I gazed after it, full of delight and longing. For that marvellous winged seed, coming from the unknown and returning to it again, seemed of the very essence of freedom and beauty: a thing softer than silk, fairer than flowers, yielding to the wind yet riding it, skimming the sea and then taken up into heaven.

When I had finished playing with the canach seed, I had a game with another wild white thing. There is an endless fascination in spume. Children, and not children alone, love soap-bubbles, even in the wash-tub, though lather has dismal associations with laundering and shaving. But spume – the useless froth of irresponsible water – is a sheer delight, from the tiniest pin-head bubble that strays at the source of a burn, to the vast heaving rafts that float under grim Atlantic cliffs, or pile up under the banks of a river in spate. It had rained in the night; and before long I came to a minute burn, where spring water had carved for itself a channel deep in the peat. Upstream on the right was a fall a few inches high, breaking the even flow, while farther down the water hurried in little rapids through a bed of rushes. Spume was forming under the fall – light spume, which floated down in rafts of varying size. In the still water between the fall and the rapids, the rafts moved slowly, disintegrating as they went, with an almost audible bursting of bubbles. But if they encountered anything solid – a leaf or twig or stem of grass to act as a nucleus – they would gather and pile up, even enlarging, till a wide pack of spume was formed, containing thousands of bubbles, gently heaving, like ice-floes on a swell. Long I knelt by the burn, steering isolated rafts by blowing across them, or making artificial ripples with a twig, which would unite them with other groups, or drive them under the bank. Or I would hurry them on towards the rapids among the rushes, where the speed of the water broke them up.

As I watched the bubbles float past in their thousands, I remembered a night spent in my tent by the river Blackwater, near Garve. I reached the place at the tail-end of a thunderstorm which had yielded over an inch of rain in a couple of hours. The level ground near the village was under water, and higher up, where the river comes down in continuous falls and rapids, shadowed by pine woods, a sullen yeasty flood poured over sheets and ledges of polished rock. Fearing more rain and perhaps a rising wind, I pitched my tent among the trees, not twenty yards from the bank, which shook with the force of the spate. The noise was so tremendous, so overpowering, that the loudest thunderclap would have passed unheard. At first it seemed an immense monotonous roar, like the lowest note of a vast organ held down indefinitely. But as I lay sleepless hour after hour, I began to distinguish overtones and undertones, as if the river were no longer one thing, but the sum of its million million racing drops of water. In listening to surf, such distinction is easy, because the waves that compose it are of varying size and strength, and each wave has its own voice. But even in the apparent monotone of rivers and streams, where at least, for the short period of listening, the volume of water passing over certain stones seems constant, the attentive ear will soon distinguish a multitude of different sounds. Spend a wakeful night in a house beside a burn, and by daybreak you will have heard not a solo but a whole choir.

As I listened to the Blackwater in spate, I realised that people who always live beside running water or breaking waves, as the Gaels do, will get the sound of it into their speech. There can be few languages more deeply influenced by the changing beauty of their surroundings than Gaelic, whose wealth and richness of sound is admitted by all.

I had with me a Gaelic Testament, in which I had been reading the Book of Revelation; and certain phrases remain in my mind, because I seem to have heard them in the water: *Bha guthanna, agus tairneanaich, agus dealanaich, agus crith-thalmhainn ann* and *A shuilean mar lasair theine . . . agus a ghuth mar thoirm mhoran uisgeachan.**

So it continued all night; and when the dawn came, wan and sullen, I went down to the river to wash. The flood was not so high now, but high enough, and the spume was amazing. In places where it could gather, in the shelter of rocks or jutting bank, it lay in piles or drifted in rafts. Out

---

* 'There were voices and thunderings, and lightnings, and an earthquake. . . . His eyes like a flame of fire, and his voice like the sound of many waters.'

in midstream were flat ledges of rock over which the torrent poured in arched bands, smooth and green as glass: and on them, globes of spume, large as footballs, came drifting down, till they were shattered in a rapid, or drawn aside to swell the huge mass that was piling up in the shelter of the west bank.

The spume rafts of the sea – and there must be thousands of acres of them round the coasts of Britain – are like those on a big river, but they have a swing and sway that can be found only on the ocean, where waves have unlimited freedom. And there is another difference. Salt spume, when newly formed, is white as one night's snow; but when drifting and gathered, it becomes yellow and even brown, like snow that has been trodden by man or beast. For it is mixed with sand churned up from the bottom, with fragments of weed and minute creatures of the sea. Seen from the cliff, the floating tracts of spume look like carpets or fleeces in which, if we dared to jump, we should sink as in feather beds, and yet be saved from drowning.

On the endless strands of the Western Isles, in calm weather, I have watched long rows of waves come in when the tide is ebbing. Each wave is fringed with foam; and as it retreats, the spume is left behind in a lacy pattern which dries and disintegrates with the bursting of millions of bubbles, and a soft hiss that rises like a descant on the even roar of the surf. If there is a strong breeze from the sea, fragments will fly inland like snowflakes, leaving a salt taste on the lips. And where a stone or heap of tangleweed forms an obstacle, spume will gather in balls, quivering, iridescent, till a puff of wind sends them spinning up the shore to dissolve among the sandhills. However airy and light it may seem, spume has a certain solidity; for even in its purest state, when snatched from the crest of a wave by wind, or even by the draught of the wave's advance, it will show dark against a bright sky.

And at length when night is near, and the last beam picks out some corrie in the Cuillins, I wander homewards, full of an unspeakable delight. Down by the shepherd's house, where the burn emerges from the tumult of its birchy gorge to seek the level floor of the strath, was once a mill, and the ground about it shows traces of lazy-bed cultivation. But the old people vanished, and Nature, with all her lovely irresponsible tribes, has reconquered her lost dominion. The derelict undrained slope is now a mass of cotton-grass and ragged robin and yellow flag. In late July and August you will find there the grass of Parnassus, with its snowy green-veined cup and starry centre, swaying on delicate stem. And perhaps a shower has left a drop of water in the spoked hollow of a young lupin leaf at my gate, shining with a sheen beyond diamonds. Through its transparency you will see the rayed pattern of the supporting leaf, changed from green to crimson, and resembling the markings on the two ends of a sea-urchin's shell.

In all these things, as I said, there is an unspeakable delight. For the whole of the wild is ours, from the river in spate to the drop at the heart of the leaf, by right of kinship and in virtue of contemplation, without purchase or conquest. We may be penniless, alone, without home or kin; but the world of Nature is ours to take, if only we have the seeing eye and understanding heart.

It was a quiet evening in June, with nothing to trouble you but the midges. We had been working all day to secure an early crop of seeds hay, and while they carted the last load, I went up to the moss to cut a few more peats. At the next bank I saw Mary from the shore. She had an old mother of ninety to look after, but managed to run her croft single-handed, shearing sheep and reaping corn, and her home with a little garden before it, kept scoured and shining as if she had nothing else in the world to do. Being tired and vexed with midges, and perhaps lazy as well, I walked across to the place where she was. Our collies growled and bristled, but we cursed them into silence, and began to talk about the uncanny drought, and the way the peats were drying without any handling at all. Then Mary said casually: 'I'm hearing that they are after taking Paris.' 'I was afraid of that,' I replied. 'Indeed yes. And isn't this an awful war?' After that we went back to the peats – how long they would need to lie before stacking, and whether Duncan would not get his cart right up to the face of the bank, as the moss was so terribly dry.

After a while I returned to my own bank and set to work. In this Highland glen, sweet with bogmyrtle and loud with the buzzing of summer flies, the war seemed a remote unreal nightmare, like the average man's conception of hell. Once indeed we heard the distant boom of naval guns: windows shook, and sheep stopped grazing to eye one another with blank surmise. I felt lonesome in my empty house, and lighted the primus stove for the sake of its loud consoling roar. But that was ages ago, on the day before they invaded Holland. Now the horror had rolled nearer, and become less like eschatology and more like a thunder-cloud rising quickly behind hills. If they were coming down the road just now, I thought, we should be feeling different. Yes – for a time. And then the patience of the peasant, his enduring and measureless stoicism, would prevail. When bombs fell in the Dutch fields, the placid black and white cows returned to graze round the craters. True, they may soon be coming down the road, and their planes droning above them. But we shall need fires next winter all the same.

The threatened coal shortage has driven many veterans back to the forsaken peat moss, and with them some novices, whose queer-shaped sods and awkwardly gashed bank-faces betray the prentice hand. The moss of Fernaig, where we work, is on the top of one of the old raised beaches of Loch Carron, where four to five feet of peat overlie a hard bottom of gravel and shingle. In days gone by, when there were many crofters and no coal, much of the surface was cut away, leaving a few heather-covered knolls and banks where peat can still be won, islanded in tracts of mossy swamp and water. Before starting to cut the peat, the top layer of heather roots must be stripped off, and the turves laid at the foot of the bank. After that, brick-shaped pieces of peat can be easily cut with the *torr-sgian* or peat knife. My own bank yields four layers of sods, the upper two being brownish and rather fibrous, while the lower ones are soft and clayey, cutting like butter, and drying to hard blocks that burn hot and slow. The newly cut peats must be spread out to dry, and the cutter is the better of an assistant to carry out the sods as fast as they are cut. Later when the upper side is dry, they are turned, and then, unless the weather is exceptionally dry, set up in little groups of four or six, like sheaves in a stook. And last of all they are stacked or carried home. Stacking, if the stack is to weather a wet winter, needs skill, and you must build a fence against roaming cattle. If you have a handy shed or barn, it is better to haul the peat home in bags while the moss is dry enough for the traffic of carts.

I had no helper, and after a spell of cutting I must carry out the peats myself and spread them on the heathery knoll behind me. I worked barefoot, for under the bank was oozy mud and water, soft and deliciously warm, as water always is in the pools of a peat moss. My sods were roughly cut, and the face of the bank was gashed and uneven, as if it were a huge chunk of butter at which a boy had been hacking with a blunt penknife. The first twenty bags were cut in exceptionally dry weather, and when filled they lay for days on the knoll, round and drab like Atlantic seals basking on a rock, until a neighbour came with a cart and hauled them home. There is no darkness here at Midsummer, and if we do not rise very early, neither do we grudge working late. It was twenty minutes past midnight when Duncan's cart rumbled through my gate. We laughed and wished each other good morning.

I worked till after sunset. Out on the loch, boats were moving up and down where the tides run strong among the islands, fishing for cuddies with rods and goose-feather flies. On the common grazing, old women herding their cows had lighted fires to keep away the midges. The faint blue smoke rose into the quiet sky, as it has risen from the beginning of the world. Spring comes late in the north, and even in this hot dry June the oaks and birches of the glen had kept their young and vivid green. The collies' coats were sweet with the bogmyrtle among which they lay asleep. The great rampart of Applecross rose dark from the sea, with night in its corries, and a thin wisp of cloud lying across the ridge of Beinn Bhan. In the west this twilight hour must always touch the heart, and now it had the intensity given to all fair things by the imminence of doom, as if our mortal eyes were looking on them for the last time.

Last spring I had a sudden vision of the glen with its few small houses in ruins. Sharp spears of young grass were thrusting upwards through the rubble, and on the edge of a bomb crater were daffodils, half buried and askew, waving their frail and gallant banners. Clouds drifted on the hills, and in the empty land a curlew cried, and water lapped on stone. If this were more than some lying trick of the imagination, it would not be the first time that Highlanders had seen their homes destroyed. Norsemen ravaged the isles, and hostile clans laid waste the glens: and almost within living memory the lairds and their factors set fire to many a crofter's thatch. But the people lived on, and rebuilt the old life in the old way. Against the new cloud rising from the east, the herdsman's fire goes up with its faint blue smoke. He may raise his eyes to watch the tanks go by: but then will turn to fill the creel with peats. For at long last, it is not the captains and the kings that count. When they have gone to dust, the fire on the poor man's hearth will still be bright.

The Old Barn at Fernaig | 1

In the Western Highlands August is a broken month. You may not see the sun for days, except as a watery blink among flying clouds; and if the sea is calm at all, it will be heaving, oily and leaden, under the rain of a slow-moving depression. Master and horse stand idle, eating their heads off, in acquiescence, perhaps even with secret pleasure. Forks and rakes are piled in the barn, or more probably lie hidden in dripping grass where the last user has thrown them down. Only Nature is quietly busy, pushing up spears of young grass through sodden swathes of hay, bringing chickweed and dockens to lush perfection, sending out armies of black shining slugs to ravage the garden. Strangers may thump the barometer, and flatten impatient noses against the rainspattered window. But we who know this country have learned a better way. We thank God for His mercy of rest-bringing rain; and leaning against the stable door-post, listen to the slow drip of water from the eaves, the roar of swollen burns, the swish of wind-vexed rowans and alders. Or we go down to the barn, and burrowing deep into the hay, fall asleep till the clouds roll by.

On such a day I went to the barn at Fernaig. It is a long narrow building with steep-pitched roof and slatted sides, probably dating from the early nineteenth century, when the glens were invaded by Lowland sheep farmers. In recent years it has been reconditioned. The tough heather thatch and wattles of plaited hazel have yielded to corrugated iron and movable wooden slats. Yet there is still an antique, almost an ecclesiastical look about the interior. The modern roof is supported by the original rafters – vast beams of rough-hewn oak, trimmed by hand and fastened with heavy wooden pegs. They must have been carefully chosen and hard to get, for each pair is built into the wall, and meets to form a pointed arch, the curve being no more than the natural shape of the limb of some great tree. A few have been replaced, and the slight machine-sawn timbers look grotesquely frail in comparison. A third of the barn is filled with a pack of hay, for in this climate ricks are rarely built outside. The rest of the floor space is occupied by a sloping wooden rack on which the half-dried hay brought in from the field gets a further curing before it is forked up with the rest.

A pile of fresh hay was lying beside the main pack, and I made myself a nest there, carefully coiling my body to avoid getting seeds and bits of stalk down my neck, for such fragments make a good substitute for a hair shirt. Outside, a blast from the south was driving before it long shafts of rain, which struck the iron roof with a drumming that rose and fell with the force of the wind. Now and again a stray gust would dart in, rattling the half-door and lifting fringes of loose hay from the rack. Birches lashed their supple branches, and revealed the shining undersides of leaves in a billowy cascade of wetness. On the moss an over-late harvest of peat stood soaking, forlorn and half immersed in surface water. The corn, a promising crop a week ago, lay flat in tangled confusion, not unlike a demoralised piece of rush matting. The hayfield was a melancholy draggle, and the lush potato shaws were sagging under the weight of water-drops. Roses and gladioli looked faded and battered, thus showing the inferior stamina of garden flowers: for on the hill, not only tough heather and stringy knapweed, but the graceful scabious and delicate grass of Parnassus accept the storm and survive it unscathed. The loch was grey and wrinkled, with short breaking waves that roared on the skerries in faint echo of the great seas beyond Skye. The Ascaig river ran dark and full beneath the alders, covering the gravel of the ford. Small burns came tumbling down the gullies in a smother of white and brown. Horses stood under the hedge with backs to the wind, their short summer coats all plastered and shining. A few adventurous hens were searching for grubs; the wind ruffled their plumage and parted it to the skin.

I had known the barn for nearly fifteen years, and the drowsy scent of the hay put me in reminiscent mood. How many things must have happened there since those great beams were first hauled into place. I thought of the generations of cattle which had eaten the stored hay, had mated and calved and yielded their milk and then gone down into silence. And after that, of the men who had laboured in hope and weariness, of lovers who once had lain there, high up on the top of the pack, in the heady fragrance. Away at the back I remembered a hole in the roof, about the size of a penny, through which a dusty sunbeam may have slanted down on a girl's bright hair. And below, on the loose hay, a tramp relaxed his old bones, and thought of the day when first, at some dull job, he saw the white road vanishing round the corner.

How many things must have happened there! And some, like the brimming tide, have left their traces behind. Even when cleared for action at harvest time, the barn contains not only bright-pronged forks and spreading rakes, but some of that treasured junk that makes a farmer's shed or loft or stable into a human museum, rich in memories of deeds and pleasures and sorrows. Near the door is a cake-crusher; above on the wires, two rods with lines spread to dry. Under the roof are coils of stack-rope, and at the north gable, slung high above our heads, an ancient worm-eaten seat, of the kind once found in every thatched house. It had been bequeathed to Bean Fhearnaig by an old woman from the township on the shore, who must have had little faith in her neighbours' kindness of heart, for she was convinced that her rheumatic twinges were caused by pins stuck into her knees by ill-wishers, and wore the lids of milk cans strapped over them as a shield against the devices of the enemy!

The summer of 1940 was not kind to us. First came a drought when nothing grew but deep-rooted weeds, and no work prospered but the peats. Even the sheep, who normally delight in dryness and need but little water, would gather daily to drink at the edge of the shrunken hill lochs. Then in July the weather broke, as it seemed for good, just as the bulk of our hay was ready for the mower. We had been able to cut a little seeds hay in June; but most of the Highland crop is not ready till late July or August, because the lambing ewes are kept on the ground till the end of May. So we embarked on a long and exhilarating fight with the rain, drying our hay on wire fences or wooden tripods, and taking loads into the barn on all but the worst days.

And on these worst days, when it is impossible to do anything outside but try for a sea-trout at the falls, it is fine to sit at ease in the barn, where everything is pleasant to look at, not least the hay itself. When the crop is dried by the wind, as happens on fence or tripod, and is little exposed to the sun's bleaching, the leaves of grass remain green, and flowering plants retain their colour, though a little subdued by desiccation. The bluish purple of vetch is there, and the reddish purple of knapweed; the yellow of hawkweed and pink of clover, all perfect as in a child's book of pressed flowers. The seeding heads of various grasses, cocksfoot and sweet vernal, foxtail and feathery meadow-grass, are all shapely and distinct, as they were when growing in the field. Their smooth cream or honey-coloured stalks are polished like straw, only less harsh to the touch. Frail seeds of various shapes drift down to the floor, where they make a soft carpet for the feet. Hay from the poorer ground is full of the gleaming parchment-like seed-vessels of the yellow-rattle, which give it a crisp rustle, and by spacing the fine grass help to dry it.

Grass everywhere – millions of stalks and heads, billions of seeds, the lavish harvest of a whole field, soon to vanish into the maw of cattle and become milk or beef. Some of these seeds will pass out of the beasts and return to the field with the dung, there to produce a new generation of grass, another crop of hay. And so on for ever. *Behold all flesh is as grass.* In a land of fierce sun, where plants spring up today and tomorrow are burnt, grass may be the fittest symbol of mortality. But in the kindly west, where vegetation grows and withers more slowly, we think less of the transient individual than of the lasting species, and so find comfort.

I picked up a handful of hay and crushed it between my fingers. It had a dampish feel, for the moisture drifting through the slats prevented the top layer from becoming crackling dry. Idly I wondered who had forked this particular handful into the cart, who had thrown it on the rack, and on what day of the coming winter it would be carried to the byre and set before the cattle. I could see with my mind's eye the shiny black heifer we called Zebo curling her tongue about it, and gradually drawing it in, till a knapweed stem, stuck jauntily out of her mouth, was all that was left of that fragrant bundle of flowering grass.

Towards sunset the drumming of rain diminished and then ceased. The light that filtered in through half-closed slats and piled hay was not enough to read by; but for a while I sat on, watching the shadows deepen among the dust and cobwebs of ages, up there in the dim rafters. The iron sheets of the roof gleamed faint like fluted silver. It is fine, I thought, to sit by yourself in a quiet enclosure, in empty church or barn or forsaken attic, and let the daylight ebb from you, slowly, inevitably, as the tides of the sea or your own life at the last, until you are left alone with the friendly and sheltering darkness. Fine to see the edge of solid things dissolve and melt into shadows and then into nothing, setting us free: to see the rampant brilliance of noon fade till it seems no more than a hint, a suggestion of sun that has gone elsewhere, and left the sky to a thousand stars.

At last I opened the door and slipped out. It had long since settled on its hinges, and grated harshly as I dragged it across the flagstones of the threshold. Away in the steading the gander was pecking at stray grains left in the hens' pail, with a broken tapping like someone signalling in Morse. I turned up towards Achmore. In the east, far down to leeward, low billowing rain-clouds rolled away, trailing their skirts on the drenched hills, which looked inky black in the wild light streaming from the west. A perfect double rainbow spanned the glen, from the birchy braes of the south to the rock-face of the north; and under this airy bridge the Ascaig river roared down in spate. A light drizzle was still falling, and the level sun made it a floating veil of gold through which the wet trees shone transfigured. I picked my way among gleaming puddles, under the drip of leaves turned back by the wind, beside a sloping telephone wire, on which bright raindrops chased each other; the bigger ones overhauled the smaller and coalesced, and then too heavy in union, fell to the ground. Above the falls, a croft house stood empty. The enclosure was overgrown and rank with weeds, and in the midst was an ancient apple tree. The small green apples were touched with that same wild light, till they shone like golden balls in some fabulous garden of Arabia.

On my way home I passed the open door of the stable. It was empty and full of shadows; but over the manger, high up on the west wall, were two narrow loopholes, through which the day's last light was seen; and across one of them, etched in black, a trail of wild briar swayed in the wind. The stable itself was in darkness, save where the hames were hanging by the stall. The inner edge, worn by friction with the collar, gleamed like polished armour. It seemed as if this homely bit of harness had drawn to itself the light of the whole sky.

From the slats of the barn, triumphing over the smell of rain-drenched earth, poured the evocative fragrance of new hay. Tears smarted behind my eyes, for I remembered the many Sunday nights when I drove home in the trap, past the hay-laden fences, and into the silent waiting steading of Achnabo, in the days that seem so good because they will never return.

Very early, when the first rays are slanting across the dewy heads of the long grasses, the farmer is afield with his mower, so that his horses can work in the cool of the dawn, and swaths may have a whole day's sun for drying. Very late, in lingering twilight and under the first stars, his loaded carts will rumble into the stackyard. But in raw January, when the setting moon is stronger than the tardy light of day, the same man may be lying in bed at nine, or if it is a frosty spell in the Western Isles, may even be breakfasting at noon. For Nature is his clock and his siren; and she is too wise to burn the candle at both ends. Except at the lifeless Poles, the longest summer sun must set at last and the highest tide must ebb. What sense is there in rising cross and cold by smoky lamplight, before the cocks crow or sleepy cattle move from the straw?

In cities they have lost this ancient wisdom. Summer and winter, in light or in darkness, in sunshine or rain, the clock is master. Alone in all creation, man can take no rest. Stars may set, but you cannot stop a machine or let out a furnace, for if you do, money will be lost or production hindered, and the weary wheel of making and spending gets jammed. If this is work, no wonder there was none in Eden. And for a long time after, when the light of dawn was still on the world, men were content to live by hunting. Danger and death were at the door, and hunger never far off, but they were free. If the morning sky were red and ragged, and a south wind moaning through bare branches, they could turn over on their heather beds and sleep till noon. Later, when flocks and herds were all their wealth, people would wander in search of pasture, as Bedouins do today, and where the grass grew rich and green beside a burn, would make their camp and rest, with none to put them out or move them on. Their lives were ruled by Nature, a stern enough mistress, but kinder than machines, industrialists, or dictators. We might do worse than serve her again.

Wild animals work hard for their living, especially those that depend on grazing. As we watch a herd of deer, or even a flock of hill sheep moving over their accustomed pastures, our first thought is that food is their main concern, and how hard they must labour to get it. For us too, food – only under some vaguer and more dignified name – is the main concern, and we too must work for it, and perhaps in less pleasant a fashion. But our second thought, if we stop long enough for that, is that this mere questing for grass to eat, with all its incidental problems, demands great intelligence, patience, and alertness, for the wild or semi-wild animal has to depend upon itself alone. Every farmer knows that the half-wild Highland or Galloway is far more intelligent than the heavily-fed dairy cow. Hens are proverbially stupid,* but it is we who have made them so. No wild bird can afford to

---

* 'Ceann circ, ceann amadain' – a hen's head is a fool's head.

be brainless, for in Nature, the wages of stupidity, as of idleness, is death. Thus it is not surprising that the general level of intelligence and resourcefulness among primitive peoples is very high, for every man's life and wellbeing depend on his own exertions. Whereas a highly developed and mechanised civilisation demands outstanding intelligence in a few at the top, and a spoon-fed acquiescence in the vast multitudes below, whose very thoughts and desires, little as they may know or admit it, are organised from above.

There is no sense in labouring this point. For long ago most thinking people came to see that mechanised civilisation was wrong, and that our wars, revolutions, and social unrest are in great part an attempt, however unconscious, to rid ourselves of this unnatural monstrosity. Few of us, if pressed, would deny this; but most of us believe that it is an evil at our present stage unavoidable, and that only as individuals can we hope to escape. And if, by twos or by threes, we do escape, they call us selfish or cowardly. To such a degree has the machine enslaved us all. It may indeed have speeded up production; but instead of giving us the right kind of leisure, it has multiplied our wants, flooding the world with useless trash that requires the vast resources of modern advertising for its distribution and sale. In Bolivia, which like the West Highlands is a land of *mañana*, an English lady once asked why some piece of work was not done in a more efficient way, as it would save so much time. '*Si, señora,*' was the polite reply, 'but what would we do with the time when we had saved it?' A profound, far-reaching question, and we might do well to ask it rather more often.

The South American gaucho, living with horses on the windy pampas, has his own way of looking at the world and at the more advanced peoples in it: and I cannot refrain from quoting some comments made by one of these men, revealing ourselves as others see us. 'Over there in Europe,' he said, 'people are mad. They think that we are brutes. But look at them, with their culture, art, fine cities, roads, and more churches than there are ranchos in the whole province of Buenos Aires. Yes, look at these Cristianos, and listen to them. All they do is to fight and talk about fighting, and billions of pesos are spent on machines of destruction. And what for? – yes, what for? All we see in the papers are pictures of huge bombers, tanks, rows and rows of soldiers, battleships, generals and admirals with many medals on their chests. And yet not one of them could ride a bronco, or do a day's work with us, without being carried off in an ambulance. Europe smells of corpses and blood. And yet they think that we are brutes. If this is all that culture has done for them, I am happy to be just a simple gaucho."

Perhaps the most interesting aspect of mechanised civilisation is the kind of morality it has produced. God loves wealth and its efficient pursuit; it is a sin to let a machine run down, and Satan will find mischief still for idle hands to do. So we must have organised work, organised food and sleep, organised play. To fall out of the ranks, to think or look at something, or do some little job your own way, is to clog the wheels of progress. The ideal type is the industrious

* Quoted by F. Tschiffely in *This Way Southward* (in 1940).

apprentice who at last, by ceaseless toil, becomes a magnate; and having been so long in harness, can find no use for his wealth and leisure but in the dreary sport of killing time. Admiration of this type has become instinctive. We often hear really good people blaming others for not striving to get on in the world, though there is little use in going full steam ahead if we are only travelling in a circle.

'There is no dust in the lark's house,' but to the termite the lark must seem a lazy, thriftless being who fiddles while Rome burns. So also to the organised worker of civilisation, the primitive man appears idle because he works in fits and starts, and lives in feast or fast. Take the Hebridean as he was even fifty years ago. He has been called lazy, but the cap fits just as much or as little as it would fit the deer of the hills or the birds of the sea. The magnate and his well-fed work-people would find plenty to grumble about if they were put in his place. Lonely on rock or bog, or overcrowded on the machair, supposing that any of this fertile land were left him by the large farmers, he was forced to turn every foot of precious soil to account. Hillsides and headlands are still ridged and seamed with the marks of laborious spade cultivation.* Isolated from the mainland, and without money to buy its products even if he could get them, the crofter was thrown back on his own resources. He must grind his

---

* Trenches were dug about 2 feet apart, and on the intervening ridges, well-manured with seaweed, potatoes were planted, and then covered with the soil taken from the trenches. This method is still employed on rocky, boggy ground where the plough cannot work. It would be interesting to know who first called these ridges lazy-beds – whoever did, had never made one. In Gaelic they are called 'feannagan'.

own corn, cut his own fuel, weave his own cloth, make most of his own implements and utensils, build and repair his own house. Nothing was wasted; when the house was re-thatched, the old roof, impregnated with peat smoke, was stripped off and used to fertilise the soil. Each man had to be a master of many trades, and so exacting a life called forth and maintained not only a spirit of endurance, but a very high level of intelligence.

In the hard seasons – the long bleak days of spring and the hot heavy days of harvest – the crofter would be early and late at work, toiling with a will, because the labour was for himself and his own people, and would not last too long without a break. For between the sowing of corn and the cutting of hay were those weeks of early summer, the loveliest period of the Highland year, when the cattle were driven to the hill pastures, and whole townships would gather sociably at the peat banks. And later, even after the most strenuous harvest, would come the peace that follows Samhain, when all was safely stored and battened down for winter. There would be hauling of peats and carting of seaweed, and no one who has handled wet tangle in the biting wind of the isles will deny that it is hard work. But the days were too short for weariness, and were rounded with long evenings at the fire, with plenty of potatoes and salt herring and oatcakes, and plenty of songs and tales. No early milking, no winter ploughing, and above all no factory sirens shrieking in the raw foggy dawn.

It is easy enough to idealise a past whose hardships are lost in the mist of distance. Life was precarious, and the margin between sufficiency and hunger very narrow. A bad harvest or an unduly prolonged winter might kill off the cattle and drive the people to the cockle strands. But I believe there was more personal freedom, more content, more gaiety of heart than there is now among those whose standard of life is infinitely higher and whose possessions are a hundredfold more numerous.*

Captain Scott, who used teams of huskies for sledging, considered that the one thing needful was to keep them interested. Above all other animals a working dog delights in his job, even welcoming the sight of his harness with the keenest pleasure. But monotony he cannot stand; and Scott found that pulling on an endless snowy plain soon finished the dog, not with fatigue but with boredom. Man is the same; and the old Highlanders understood the heartening value of communal work and of labour songs. The former still persists, and can be seen in every township at the peats or at the potatoes. But the songs have gone from the fields and byres, and are now to be heard only at concerts or ceilidhs. Hand weaving has been revived, especially in Lewis and Harris, but the cloth is shrunk at the mill, and the fine old *orain luadhaidh* or waulking songs are heard no more. This is a pity, for not only has the hand-finished cloth a better appearance, but the waulking itself, which was a useful piece of work, an entertainment for the bystanders,

---

* Only the other day a woman of forty in Lochbroom said to me, 'They had more fun in those days than we do now. Look how the boats that went to the islands for shell sand used to race each other home!'

and an emotional outlet for the workers, is a thing unique in the history of labour.

All this has gone beyond recall. And if people now accuse the Hebridean of laziness, it is not always easy to refute the charge. But the fault is not his. The old spirit of independence, the wholesome dislike of working at fixed hours for a master, still persists, and so does the timelessness of the west, the soft climate, the hypnotising croon of the sea. But the islesman is no longer face to face with a stern but stimulating necessity. The Government has at last realised its duty to our remote Atlantic fringes; but like a modern parent, has only laid down the cane to pick up the toffee tin. Spoon-feeding the people is the great sin and folly of all democracies; and to southern eyes, so often blinded by ignorance or false sentiment, conditions seem much worse than they really are. Over-production on the mainland has cast up a mass of cheap trash on the shores of the furthest isles, which pensions and children's earnings now enable the people to buy. Before the war the number of commercial travellers visiting the small merchants of the Western Isles was incredible, especially when their expenses per £100 worth of goods sold must have been the highest in Britain.

What has been gained? Better medical services, better education, quicker communications – all to the good. The housing subsidy has proved a more doubtful blessing. The new houses are larger, roomier, lighter: but most of them are cold and draughty. Apart from the stone, they are built of mass-produced imported material – asbestos tiles, corrugated iron, concrete blocks, cheap woodwork. To enter an old thatched house in a storm was like stepping into the stillness and security of a cave. In the new one, your feet are cold with scurrying draughts and your ears deafened with the rattle and clang of ill-fitting windows and tiles too light for their work. People go clad in the shoddy, flimsy clothes and shoes provided by mail-order stores, while the tweeds, if still made, are sold for export. In Barra, the construction of the new road and the traffic of lorries it encourages has induced many crofters to give up peats in favour of expensive coal which must be paid for in money and requires a closed range. It is easy to theorise, but the Government might have done better to concentrate on the provision of holdings, the adequate protection of the fisheries, and the lowering or even complete abolition of outward freights, thus encouraging the export of livestock and other agricultural produce.

The price paid for coming into line with the mainland has been heavy; but it may not be too late to undo the worst mischief. Old traditions have persisted so long that there are many people of no great age who remember them and regret their passing. The islanders have still more independence of life and action, are less given to mass thinking than the people of the mainland. Gaelic has not yet lost its hold among the young. What propaganda could never have achieved may be taught by stern necessity, for crofters are coming to realise that their old self-sufficient economy would have tided them over the war, and that for many years to come the Government will not have a penny to spend on the Hebrides.

The islands have a great opportunity. Free from the curse of industrialism, and comparatively unspoilt by rich sporting interests, they might become a place where people could have happy and kindly lives without extremes of wealth or poverty, with plenty of healthy work and natural amusement.

In mid-July the corn stood erect as the serried spears of an
immense host. A scorching June had rushed it into ear, and
following rains had come to swell it: and now the dark green
forest rustled with promise, swaying on stems that soon
would bear the weight of a plundering chaffinch. 'This year',
we thought, 'it will never go down on us.' But it did, and
badly too. Before the first tinge of yellow crept over the field,
there came a string of drizzling days, without wind to scatter
the gathered drops, till the heads of corn, gemmed beyond
bearing, drooped limply, and the stem, with its unprofitable
burden, bent and sank to the ground. Wind came then, but
too late and much too strong. It poured over the southern
ramparts of the glen and crashed in vertical gusts upon the
corn, leaving it lying in curious plaits and circles. For the
seaward end of the glen, where the corn was sown that year,
is flanked by a great rock, the eastern spur of a line of crags
a thousand feet high, which fall in precipice and steepest
slope to the loch below. Often from the rock itself or from a
boat I have seen blasts swooping down from above upon the
water, so that catspaws flew out in every direction, like the
darting cracks that open when ice or glass receives a straight
blow. There is no doubt that the same thing happened to the
corn. For later on, when I went to set up some fallen stooks,

I found several lying spread-eagled, with all eight sheaves pointing in different directions, as if they had been lifted and deliberately dropped to form a star. These stooks were all at the bottom of the field, and under the rock.

And so, when the corn was ready for cutting, it lay in a twisted carpet all over the field, with here and there a few stems standing to measure the disaster. Labour was scarce, and we meant to cut the crop with a one-horse mower. But no machine could work in that mess, so we borrowed two men from the Forestry Commission, and a tinker with his young son from the encampment at the crossroads, and provided them with scythes. But the young men of today, even supposing that they can use a scythe at all, have none of the skill of their fathers; and if the scythe will not cut to their liking, never think of seeking the cause in themselves, but find the set wrong, or the wedge too loose, or the handle too short or too long, and as much time is wasted in hammering and argument as would suffice to mow the whole field. At last the Laird took away one of the scythes to put a new wedge in it, while the company, having cut a few strokes, fell into one of those endless Gaelic conversations which are as the unrationed jam between thin slices of work. Only the boy, who was young enough to find pleasure in any kind of physical activity, went on binding sheaves and bringing them to me for stooking. After a while the Laird's head was seen bobbing along the ridge, and the talk drifted into English and died.

Work was resumed, but not for long. There was a call from the steading, and the men trooped in to dinner in the farmhouse kitchen. On the big scoured table bowls of broth were steaming, flanked by plates of sliced Glasgow bread. But no cups adorned the board, nor was there any teapot stewing on the hob. After a few minutes of hopeful patient waiting, the reapers filed out again, unsugared and uncheered. This wretched business of tea-rationing has brought the war into every crofter's home, and put the most rheumatic old woman into the firing line. It is the doom of hospitality, the traveller's despair, the canker at the heart of the ceilidh. When I think of all the cups of tea I have drunk through the length and breadth of the Highlands, of the black strength that was in them and the sugary syrup at the bottom, I begin to wonder if this war is worthwhile.

So out once more, but not for long, for the hills of Skye were already lost in advancing rain – perhaps a shower, but most likely the vanguard of another wet spell. Twenty minutes later the company, in acquiescence if not with relief, dispersed for good, leaving the Laird's wife to bewail a dinner given for so little. The next day without rain – for by this time we had ceased hoping for the east wind that alone could make the prostrate corn really dry – was quite naturally seized upon by the shepherd for dipping. Forty years of herding had given him the specialist's outlook, and all roads led to the fank, which on a sheep farm dominates not only the landscape but the hearts of men. He had absorbed all available labour, including the master's eye. But tinkers rarely work with sheep, and word was sent for them to come as early as possible.

The day wore on, and not a tinker in sight. There had been a wedding among them, when bride and bridegroom, arrayed in miscellaneous glories, marched from camp to church with a piper going before: and this was followed by prolonged jollifications at the village inn, in which our reapers, being closely related to the bride, took no small share.

The empty cornfield gleamed in the sun, inviting to work, in spite of its wretched condition. Part was a ragged stubble, looking as if it had been grazed by a bison in a hurry, and cumbered with a crowd of drooping cock-eyed stooks: while the rest was a trailing carpet of stems prostrate but unsevered. I found a scythe thrown down at the verge, and beside it a stone. Giving the blade a hopeful rub, I began to mow.

Now there is no more delightful, no more invigorating work than the mowing of standing corn, with a good breeze from behind to bend the stems to the blade; and nothing more charming to eye and ear than the swishing rustle of straw, the musical ring of razor-sharp edge, the gleam of sunbeam on steel, and the delicate scrape of the whetstone, which holds, like the wild bee's drone, all summer in its sound. Gallantly you advance in slow swinging rhythm, leaving an ordered polished swath behind, as a spider in motion pays out her shining thread. The beauty of scything lies in its curves – the open () of the blade faintly repeated in its track on the ground, and the gracious sweep of well-spaced parallel swaths. But here was another story. The tangled corn lay all about my feet, and I must force the blade under the mat, only to find it clogged with a yielding mass of wet rotting stalks, with ears delicately sprouting into white or tenderest green. I was never able to cut more than three or four successive strokes in any direction, never able to lay out a swath that anyone could bind into well-bottomed sheaves. The action was mere hacking, as of one who mows tough bracken, and the result was like cutting the nails of one's right hand with a very blunt pair of scissors.

But I moved on, with pauses to bind and stook what I had cut, and other more frequent pauses to sharpen the scythe. In such back-straightening moments there was plenty to look at. The Laird's brother-in-law, who was born in this country, used to quote, not without personal application, a Gaelic proverb which says that the bad reaper has long sight, and this, like many another saying of the same sort, is only too true. To be able to look about you is the solace of much outdoor work, which might otherwise be as tedious as sweeping the stairs with no staircase window.

On the brae above the shepherd's house I could see the fank, with its stone enclosures packed with sheep, and figures of men moving to and fro, and lissom collies sitting on dykes or barking in circles outside. On the far side of the river was another cornfield, belonging to an old fellow lately home from Patagonia, who, wishing to free himself from the helpfulness of neighbours and the indolence of tinkers, bought a brand-new binder. Our daily excitement was to look east 'to see if M—'s binder had gone out yet'. According to the Laird, you must have at least 30 acres to cut and 3 heavy horses to make a binder pay for itself, whereas poor M— had only 5½ acres and 2 Highland ponies. We reckoned that the price paid for his Juggernaut would have provided him with armies of tinkers for several years, and allowed them to break a good many scythes as well. When the binder did go out, it cut only a very few rounds, because it was as much as the ponies could do to pull it empty; and we were left wondering if he would ever be able to haul it out of the place where it was, or whether Nature would gradually bury it in nettles and oblivion, as is her way with human follies and failures.

And when tired of man, I could watch the tide rising and falling on the skerries, and hear the lonely cry of a raven far up in the sky, calling my thoughts to the wild life of the hill, to the gleam of lilies on hidden lochs, and the blown flame of a tinker's fire in the night. A cold, poor, dirty life, without gathering into barns, but free as air, and full of the careless rapture of birds. So Deirdre lived in Glendaruel with the sons of Usna.

I mowed away with a light heart, drawing a perverse pleasure, such as in youth can be found in shocking one's elders, from the practice of a craft thought unfit for a woman. I have often wondered why one is allowed to lift the heaviest pails of potatoes, or tend the fiercest and most treacherous cattle, and yet may not cut standing corn with a scythe or clip the meekest ewe. Can it be because these latter jobs are skilled and interesting? Scything is at least a free man's work, done with head erect and eyes above ground level, and the brightness of danger lurks in the razor-sharp blade. Surely, they say, it must be very tiring. But no one need tire at scything, if the blade is kept sharp and not allowed to drag. The handle too should be held loosely, almost negligently, and not as the novice does, with the frenzied grip of a drowning man, for only thus can the implement work unforced and of its own strength. A carpenter, when consulted about the choice of a saw, once said to me: 'You ladies should never get light tools – they must have strength behind them. The heavier ones do the job of their own weight.'

As time went on, I became a little conscious of my solitude. Mowing, like most other acts of primitive husbandry, is a communal affair. In a fair-sized field, three or four scythes will be at work, swinging in unison with a rhythm as fair as that of well-timed rowing, if not fairer; for the curve of the blade itself, and the angle it makes with the handles, and the graceful swing of the mower's body, are in themselves as full of beauty as any artist could wish. There would also be several binders working behind them, and perhaps another man stooking, and a few dogs, those happy carefree pensioners, lying about asleep – no Adam's curse for them. But now there was only one woman and one dog, and he growing old and curled into a tight wind-proof ball in the lee of the dyke.

I heard the river murmuring over the stones, and the cluck and gurgle of the tide in the weed at the sea's edge. Leaves rustled in the oak wood as a sudden breeze came in from Skye, and ewes waiting their turn at the dipper called anxiously to half-weaned lambs grown independent. The field, though partly cut, still looked so large, and myself alone with my scythe, so small, like a fly on a plate-glass window. To Wordsworth's Highland lass this acre plot of ours would have seemed a prairie. For she, more than a century ago in the Western Isles, would have been working with a sickle in a patch of grey oats or barley no bigger than a rich man's carpet, hidden away among rocks, and dug in spring with the cas chrom, in places where no horse could move nor plough turn. She would be there alone, because her man was away on the sea or at the wars, and the harvest of these little crofts must be gathered in by women. To handle the corran was as much her work as herding or spinning, and the ripe straw, with its queer seductive smell, as close to her heart as the greasy feel of yarn on the spindle or the peat-reek drifting among the rough-hewn rafters. That lonely figure, standing in meditation or defiance against an immensity of sea, has captured the imagination of thousands, as if symbolic of some Paradise lost or undiscovered, that might be reached through one of those white gates that stand ajar at nightfall. Yet her descendants are still to be found in the islands and in remote corners of the mainland, and her songs, or their like, plaintive and timeless as the wind, can still be heard whistled by boys at the hay, or hummed by the tinkers as they lift the potatoes that spout from the drill plough like foam from a ship's bows. Only in those days the corn was threshed with a flail and ground in a quern for human food, and when it gave out at the back end of winter, you tightened your belt and went gathering cockles on the shore. Whereas now there is condensed milk and tinned salmon and a pension or a remittance from abroad to tide us over the lean dark months. But under a modernised exterior the old things live on, and this business of reaping, even when the corn is fed in the sheaf to cattle, stirs ancient hopes and immemorial fears that reach back into the shadows of pre-history, to the beginning of all ages.

The dipping was over, and sheep, released from the fank, were streaming uphill like a long pale snake, guided by circling dogs. The chorus of families united, bass and treble, came down in fitful cadence, like the noise of a waterfall borne on the wind. There was an ache in my shoulder, caused by forcing the blade under the prostrate mat, and an ache in my back from stooping to sort the dry corn from the rotten, so that I was not sorry to see the Laird coming with another scythe. The sun was near setting, and its level rays, shooting out from behind the dark hill above Toscaig in Applecross, kindled the stooks to an incredibly tawny richness, as if the whole world's gold had been poured into an acre of Highland corn. Beyond, the pale expanse of loch, crisped by a wandering puff of wind, turned to a deep purplish blue. We were binding the last few sheaves when two figures appeared on the road, tacking uncertainly from side to side. It was the tinkers, returning from the village with empty pockets and a good few drams inside them. We were pleased to have managed without them; and they, sleeping off the effects by the dying camp fire, would never regret the wages and the backache they had missed. Shouldering the scythes, we sauntered home to supper.

The other day I went down the garden to put a net over the ripening raspberries. A sleek blackbird flew out, leaving behind the stripped white centre of a berry. I gave him a sour look. He had never worked in his life, yet there he was, taking the firstfruits, as if he were the rightful lord of the harvest. Not a stroke of work, but singing only, and that for his own pleasure. I was angry and a bit envious too. True, he had gone hungry last winter, and but for our dole of grain and crumbs, he must have died. But that was his life – dearth and plenty, feast and fast – and always freedom. I shook out the net. It was hard to find a sound piece, for mice had nibbled it, using the loose strands to line their nests. I was wondering if this also were a symbol, when I heard a grinding of wheels on the road. A tinker family was on the trek, the man leading a glossy pony with smart harness. The high light cart was loaded with women, children, and gear. They passed the gate without stopping, for there is an unwritten law that those who give work to the men will not be troubled with the begging and selling of the women.

From time to time there is a great movement among tinkers, which seems to come not by plan but by instinct, like the

* 'Bho'n laimh gus am beul, cuibhrionn a's fhearr air bith.'

migration of birds. Suddenly the roads are alive with creaking wheels, and mushroom tents go up in the night, flanked by a tethered pony and a cart with shafts in the air. From the dark smoky interior you may hear that cultured voice we all listen to, for many a tent has its portable set, and an aerial made of hazel sticks lashed together.

The Highland tinkers are not gipsies. They are not specially dark-skinned, and speak not Romany but Gaelic. Perhaps they are descended from landless clansmen, who had a natural taste for the wandering life, and transmitted it to their children. Many of them bear the royal name of Stewart, and someone has suggested that it was deliberately chosen as a token of respectability. But this is surely wrong. The Stewarts were unfortunate, God knows, but they could afford to leave respectability to their opponents. For did they not reach their finest flower of romance in a Prince on the run, who must have been often unshaven, and with no better sponge than a handful of moss in a sun-warmed bog-pool? In the Highlands there is no shame in frayed and faded garments, as appears in the old saying, 'A patch is better than a hole, but a hole is more gentlemanly'. Even today it might be worth losing a throne to exchange the deadly routine of constitutional royalty for the bright and battered splendours of kings in hiding.

At the same time, the Highlander does not idealise tinkers. In a poor country the struggle to settle and possess is too hard, and the line between nomad and peasant too thin for such a thought. It is in rich lands such as England that books like *Lavengro* are written and read. It is in an English folk-song that the high-born lady runs away with the Wraggle-Taggle Gipsies, and exclaims:

'What care I for a goose-feather bed,
  With the sheet turned down so bravely, O?
For to-night I shall sleep in a cold open field,
  Along with the wraggle-taggle gipsies, O!'

And much piquancy is given to Walter Starkie's gipsy fiddlings by the very fact that in term-time – I had almost said in real life – he is a university professor.

We gird at tinkers, and if we envy them, it is in irony or in secret. Yet the nomad tradition is a fine one, old as the world, and destined to last as long as men love freedom and the white road vanishing round the corner. It breeds resource and stoic acceptance and individualism, and these things are the salt of life. During the last war a tinker was called up. Official fighting was not in his line, and he took to the hill. But he was caught, and in due course sent to France, where he won the VC.

Tinkers have no stock but their ponies; yet the life they lead is a simplified pastoralism. Men like the ancient Irish or the modern Bedouin must needs be ever on the move in search of grazing. Doughty describes how the desert Arabs would debate each morning whether they should strike camp or stay where they were. If clouds were seen on the horizon, they would move after them, for clouds mean rain, and rain means fresh pasture, and water and food.

We need not travel far into Gaelic legend and history to find captains and kings living in the same hand-to-mouth fashion. Sometimes they had immense feasts lasting for several days, and then nothing. Their lavishness was unchecked by any thought for the morrow. It was said that if Fionn had as much gold as there were leaves on the trees, he would give it all away. Even nowadays prodigality is good for the reputation: it is better – or rather more gentlemanly – to spend your last pound than to save your first penny. Fionn and his companions lived by the chase: when their hunting was good they feasted like kings, and when it was bad they fell to gathering shellfish on the shore. This must have given a zest unknown to the modern sportsman, who will return empty-handed and yet expect (and get) an equally sumptuous dinner.

When clans were broken up and professional bards dispersed, the legendary stories lingered on among the people, and were handed down in the popular form they take in Campbell's *West Highland Tales*. The characters, stripped of heroic dignity, were presented as what in truth they must have been, a set of jolly vagabonds. Take the story of Diarmaid and Grainne as told by Campbell. Fionn married Grainne, daughter of Cormac, king of Ireland, and gave a wedding-feast that lasted seven days and seven nights, and afterwards there was a feast for the dogs. Among the guests was Diarmaid who had a magic mole on his face, which would make any woman that saw it fall in love with him. To avoid trouble, Diarmaid always kept his cap pulled down over the mole. But the dogs started fighting over their feast, and Diarmaid, rushing to separate them, dropped his cap, so that Grainne saw the mole and at once fell in love with its owner. She tried to persuade Diarmaid to run away with her, but he remained loyal to his friend, until at last she overcame his scruples by stratagem. They fled to the hill, where they lived not by hunting but by hawking. Diarmaid, who was a clever joiner, made wooden bowls, and Grainne went through the glens selling them. It was the shavings floating down the burn that betrayed the guilty pair to their pursuers. For Fionn recognised the shavings of Diarmaid, and let out a great Fenian cry that lured him to his death.

There is something intriguing in the thought of the High King's daughter tramping the glens with her load of bowls for sale. The story-teller saw nothing unseemly in it, and neither need we. Like Deirdre, like Charles Stewart, Grainne is on the run, and must live as she can; and we like her none the worse for that. 'You tink' is a term of abuse, but beside it is the curious saying *Comunn mo ghaoil, comunn nan ceard* (My favourite company is the company of tinkers). The man of the tent, like all travellers, has plenty of stories; he owns no master, and works when and where he pleases; his is the rank conferred by the hole that is more distinguished than the patch. We may love justice and security, but at bottom the emotion is a cold one, like the homage offered to modern plumbing. If it were not, we should not all have a sneaking admiration for the man on the road or on the run, who waves his banner of independence, no matter how ragged.

And so when that blackbird comes back for a few more berries, I may not be so hard on him.

The day was already far spent when we pulled down the old black dinghy and went out with the last of the flood. By the time we reached the bank it was slack water, with little hope of fish till the turn of the tide. But in these final days of a harvest snatched from the jaws of storm, it was not easy for us to adjust the conflicting claims of work and meals and daylight and tides: and so, with the patience that is often the lazy man's virtue, we settled ourselves to wait for the right moment. We had bamboo rods with home-made goose-feather flies intended for cuddies, or an occasional small lythe or mackerel, and hand lines baited with glittering metal 'spoons', with which we hoped to attract something larger. A plank was laid above the after-thwart, resting on the gunwale, from which Murdoch, well raised and facing the stern, could handle the rods and attend to the lines. We found the correct bearings for the bank, and rowing up and down in a small space, kept the last house of Ardineaskin on the beam, and the old lighthouse of Rudha Mor in line with the most northerly point of the nearest Strome island.

The tide had covered all the lower skerries, and was brimming to the grass of the isles, leaving a trail of birch leaves and twigs and seaweed on the brilliant guano-fed herbage. The pull of the sea on the boat had ceased, and I was rowing only to keep the lines taut. On this first night of October, the sun was setting almost directly in the west, in the gap between the northern end of the Cuillins and the high basaltic ridges towards Portree. There was a fiery glow between bars of cloud as if from a furnace in mid-Atlantic. The Cuillins themselves were hidden in those veils of whitish mist that in calm weather are sucked upward and drawn closely over the ridges of corries and over the tops of the high hills. The little houses on the shore, that hold the light so long with their whiteness, were fading into the indeterminate grey of night. At Leac-an-Aiseig, a lamp flashed out suddenly in a cottage window and was as instantly obscured. This was the only sign of war in all that quiet land. In mid-loch, a flotilla of eiderduck lay motionless, softly crooning. Now and then a flight of black-and-white drakes skimmed the water with rapid beat of wings. A few yards from the boat a seal rose, looked at us with sad intent gaze, and vanished. There was no wind at all, and no ripple anywhere.

For six hours the tide had been flowing swiftly, irresistibly, as if the whole Atlantic, swirling round the two ends of Skye, were pouring into the loch to drown it. But now we had come to that breathless and mysterious lull that precedes the first stirrings of the ebb. A moment of completion, and at the same time of intense excitement, as if the sea might pass, by the fraction of an inch, its appointed limit, and flood the whole world. The tide would be up the Ascaig river now, stemming its flow, hushing its murmur over stones, leaving a trail of seaweed among rushes and wild iris in the low pastures. Many a time I have seen the full moon of the spring tides mirrored in that transient loch of water half fresh, half salt; and leaning over the bridge, I have dropped grains of sand into the sleeping current to see if the ebb had begun.

There was no need to do more than keep the boat moving, and the brooding stillness made me dip the oars softly, so that there might be no thud of rowlocks nor splash of broken water – nothing but the drip from the blades, and the faint hiss of minute eddies chasing each other astern. But for an occasional curt order or comment, no word passed between us. At sea there is little incentive to talk: in rough weather you are driven by work and deafened by noise, while in calm, especially at night, it is as if some overwhelming authority had laid a hand on your lips. For once an anchor is raised, or even the mooring rope of a little boat cast off, we float off in detachment, almost as spirits leaving the body. We were not half a mile from the home shore, within sight of our newly thatched stack of corn, our rain-drenched hay on the fence, the potatoes with withered shaws all ready for lifting. Yet our hearts were not with them; for all we cared they might have belonged to anyone. He who embarks of his own will and pleasure belongs to the sea in life and perhaps in death. And now we were deeply conscious of this; for at the spring tides, especially at the great movements of the equinox, the sea makes us feel its immense power, even in the farthest recesses of the narrowest loch among the hills.

At last, as the fires behind Skye died down and daylight ebbed from the world, a change, at first imperceptible but ever gathering momentum, came over the face of the loch. It was as if a hand were gripping the boat from below and drawing it out to the deep. Up and down we rowed on the old beat: but when we turned east there was a babble of opposing water at the prow, and the taut lines twanged like harp-strings. And when we turned west, we felt a yielding, swaying movement, and I had to quicken my stroke to keep a strain on the drifting lines. The water in the narrows of Strome was marbled with faint swirls and eddies, delicate as the chasing on ancient steel. Winding across the middle of the strait was a well-defined current, a stream within a stream, carrying trails of weed and bubbles of spume. In crossing it we were conscious of a slight oscillation of the boat. At the western end of one of the isles, where currents met in shallow water, was a tide-rip, with leaping wavelets, a miniature Corrievreckan – rather a sinister place, for all its tiny compass.

It was then that the fish began to take. I could not see the lines, nor my companion's hands at work; but I could tell from the tension of his back and arms whether it was a fish he had got or only a trail of weed to be cleared. He hauled in cuddy after cuddy, plump and sleek, with white bellies and dark backs, and gleaming bronze lythe, and shining mackerel – the bonniest fish in the sea, especially when you see it shimmering like opal and silver as it is drawn through the water under the gunwale. Up and down we went, pulling against the tide, or skimming with it, until we reckoned that if we did not make for home at once, it would be too dark for a tidy landing. So I turned from the bank, and pulled a long steady stroke, while Murdoch hauled in the lines and sorted his rods. The dying gleam in the west could hardly touch the face of the waters, now darkened by a slowly expanding tract of ripple. Eastward, the soft clouds parted to show a few dim stars. As we approached the shore, a drift of peat smoke from the cottage of Cladach Fhearnaig greeted us with its haunting reek, and a wide band of shining wet pebbles revealed the swiftness of the ebb. As the keel grated, a lean cat stole out of the shadows and rubbed against our legs. But in vain, for our catch was too small and ourselves too lazy to be gutting the fish at the sea's edge.

We sauntered up the road to the farm, carrying the oars and the tackle, and the fish strung on a cord, with a little talk, and a good deal of thought of the cup of tea that was awaiting us. On the empty shore the tide would ebb till the small hours, as if the whole loch were pouring after the vanished sun, and its basin drained as a stranded boat when the plug is drawn. But no one would see it, for the nights were dark now, and the slip of a new moon long since set. Even the horses, who loved to roam among the pools and slippery stones of the great ebb, would not find their way down in the shadows, and the faint innumerable hissings and poppings of exposed tangle-weed would go unheard of any creature of the land.

I took a pan from the shelf and slithered down the brae in
search of the little black cow. Outdoor milking is a pleasant
job, and perhaps the best service I could offer my hosts. For
if you are a guest on a small island, or indeed in any wild
place, you must make yourself useful in some way or you
will not be asked again. Nor is a weekend visitor particularly
welcome. 'The man who comes late on Saturday,' says an old
rhyme, 'and leaves early on Monday, as far as his help goes,
I would rather he stopped away.'* The cow was not even
ours except by right of temporary hire. She belonged to the
crofter fisherman who owned most of the island, and kept
there a dozen miscellaneous cattle, headed by a sad-eyed
brown bull of no particular breed. An islander must have a
bull, for he cannot be always ferrying his cows to the mainland for service; and the simplest if not the best way is to
keep one of his own male calves. The rest of the herd were
equally mixed. There was a dun Highlander with long horns,
and a black heifer with no horns, and two black stirks with
white socks, and our own cow, black also, with furry ears

---

*   'Am fear a thig anmoch Di-sathurna
    Is a dh'fhalbhas moch Di-luain,
    B'fhearr airson a chuideachaidh
    An duine sin a dh'fhuireach bhuam.'

and a white belly and trim little feet and grey teats soft as the fingers of a kid glove. The bull ran with the cows all the year round, and there was a general calving in spring. Each cow got whatever management seemed easiest at the moment – sucking or milking or a mixture of the two, where calf and milker, one on each side, fought an unequal battle for the produce. Island cows, like their owners, are individualists, with personal likes and dislikes which it pays to study. Few care to be milked by men, and many will suffer only one woman, and woe betide the rest if that woman falls ill or dies.

Fortunately the little black cow was not so particular. She never lifted a leg or flicked her tail in your eye; but beyond this, she had little consideration for my comfort. She would watch me coming with mild, inquisitive eyes: if she were chewing her cud, she might stand till the milking was finished; but if grazing, she would never stay long enough for me to get more than five or six squirts in succession. She was no bigger than a Jersey, so that I had a long way to stoop, nor was it possible to kneel. My right hand drew warmth from the teat, but the left was cold and stiff with grasping the handle of the pan. However wet or windy the day, the hardy little beast never sought shelter for herself nor offered it to me. Yet I enjoyed the job; it reminded me of the days when I kept cows myself, and if visitors were seen approaching, someone would run out to get an extra drop from Red Anne, who always stood to be milked in the field. It was already November, and the little cow was getting nothing but rough grass; but she gave us the half-gallon we needed, and we were content.

The cattle had the run of most of the isle, but at this time of year they were usually to be found on the low promontory of Ardnagoine, which faces north-east towards the mainland. Here there was plenty of grass, for the lord of Tanera had kept the place closed all summer to provide keep at the back-end. The rank herbage must have been rich and sweet in its prime; but now it was trampled and sodden, full of the bleached and desiccated stems of foxglove and knapweed and wild parsnip, which would rustle harshly through the winter gales, till the young generations sprang forth and bore them down.

The year was far spent, and the mornings had grown very dark, so that the cow was not milked till after breakfast. A long dry autumn had broken in gales and rain, and we were getting too much of the south-east. This is a bad wind on Tanera. It comes in puffy gusts from the high hills at the head of Loch Broom, raising a nasty sea among the isles, especially when it meets a flood tide or a groundswell rolling in from the Atlantic. It blows full on the front of the stark little schoolhouse in which we were then camped, shrieking through chinks and raising clouds of peat ash from the hearth.

I opened the door with care and slipped out. The wind rushed in with a yell. There was a tussle, in which the door was victoriously closed, and the yell changed to a sullen whine in the keyhole. Pan in hand I skidded down the slippery brae. Scudding dirty clouds, twisted into curls and streamers, let fall a hard-wrung spatter of rain. There was a pallid drifty look on Beinn Mor Coigeach, which spoke of

snow not far away, and a wintry chill in the off-shore gusts.
The white croft houses of Achiltibuie were strung out in a
long line, ending in the ugly new pier at Badantarbert, which
stands there empty of life, from one rare steamer's visit to
the next. Behind was a vacant stretch of moor, with watery
gleams of sunshine running over it, and beyond that the
fantastic isolated peaks of Suilven and Stack Polly. The strait
lay wrinkled and grey, fanged here and there with white
water, and steep quick waves were breaking at my feet with
a snarl and a hiss. The little cow stood with her back to the
blast, and the long black hairs of her switch, which reached
nearly to the ground, blew between her legs and into the
milk. The wind made her restless, and she would not let me
get more than four or five successive squirts. I cursed her
heartily in Gaelic and English. No milking croons for me
at such a time. 'Ho ro, my little black heifer' is all very well
on a fine summer's evening, or when your cow is safely tied
in a byre. But on Ardnagoine in a south-easter, 'Stand, you
trash!' is more to the point.

As I trotted after my charge, I began to speculate about
the weather. Our weekly mail had failed to come on the day
appointed owing to north-westerly squalls at the tail of a
depression. Now the backing wind and falling barometer
suggested that a new one was on its way. Not only was the
mail-bag waiting at Badantarbert, but also a parcel of meat
and a newly-charged wireless battery. The postman had
an outboard engine, but this, like most Highland engines
on nearly all occasions, had broken down; and if it were
likely to blow, he would not trust to the oars. We might go

ourselves with the launch, but we wondered if it were worth the loss of working time and the expenditure of precious petrol, and whether it might not discourage the postman from coming another day. We could easily, even cheerfully, go without letters, or meat or news. The battery we had was on its last legs. It would yield just one sentence of the Nine o'Clock News before it faded, and we became skilled in gauging the moment when we might hear something important. We wanted facts, and if we hit on mere propaganda or the doings of royalty, we promptly switched off. It is surprising how many things you can forgo and never miss. And the result is not a mere vacancy, for other things come in, and mostly better ones.

This point of Ardnagoine, so fair in its low grassy levels, had the charm of fertility, real or potential, in the lap of wild ocean, which gives to small Atlantic isles their unique appeal. Yet the place always made me sad. And the feeling I had was not the tender melancholy of the west, which is not sorrow at all, but rather an exquisite pleasure – for unlike more passionate delights, it can always be prolonged and recaptured in the place that evokes it – but a sadness which, whether we like it or not, must pursue us wherever we go in the Highlands today. Every glen, every shore is strewn with wreckage left by the ebbing tide of man's fruitful and contented life in the land of his fathers. Only to a warped mind do ruins seem romantic; Nature, with more sense and compassion, does her best to hide them. Here in the small isles, where masonry is solid and invading vegetation stunted by wind, the process of healing and obliteration takes longer. Once on a brae in South Uist, I found a recently abandoned 'black house'. The heather thatch and sods underlying it had been stripped, no doubt for the sake of the rafters, which in that treeless island might be used for some other purpose. But the walls and hearth were intact, and furniture still standing in place – a wooden settle and chairs and stools, even a kettle and a few spoons. These few forlorn possessions, abandoned not by force but of someone's free will, and not yet weathered by rain, were symbolic of much beyond themselves. There was a burn beside the house, but it was a long way from the road.

The crofts of Tanera were abandoned between 1927 and 1932, in the wave of evacuation that followed the last war. The failure of inshore fishing was the main cause, for the island could not support a population depending on crofting alone. The soil on the Torridonian sandstone is thin, and has been further depleted by the ruthless cutting of peat for the former curing factory. And then the old story – the stealthy invasion from without, the willing response, and all that follows where primitive life lingers on the fringe of an industrial civilisation. 'Blue are the hills that are far from us.' The young men go in search of work or pleasure, the girls refuse to face the hardship and monotony of island days. Only the old remain, to become daily less able to do the needful jobs and maintain an independent and self-sufficient way of life. And there is irony in the thought that wireless and improved transport, which should have done so much to ease the burden of lonely communities, seem only to have increased and vocalised their discontent.

When several families have gone, it is only a matter of time till the others follow, for successful island life depends on adequate manpower, if only for transport. Stores must be carried to and from the boats; and quite apart from oars and sails, a motor launch requires a man's strength to swing the starting handle and to haul the anchor. Even a dinghy, whether afloat at moorings or pulled up above the tide-mark, needs constant and muscular attention. This we were to learn to our cost when the only man of our party broke his leg, not in any feat of cragsmanship, but when walking down a muddy slope in gumboots, looking for the little black cow. It was a simple fracture, and we set the limb in splints made out of an old packing-case. A doctor friend, who turned up later, remarked that it could not have mended better if he had fallen on the steps of a hospital. But in the days and weeks that followed this mishap, the more strenuous jobs, such as rebuilding the pier or ferrying sheep, had to be abandoned. We two women discovered that we could visit the mainland only on calm days, and must time our return for high water, so that the dinghy would need the minimum of hauling on the shore. In vain we reminded ourselves that Eskimo girls are as strong as their mates, and that female porters at Darjeeling are said to handle grand pianos as if they were deck-chairs. Too many generations of playing pianos instead of carrying them lie between us and that wild equality of strength. We would row across as quickly as possible, and then rush through our business with one eye on the sea. If white horses appeared, or the wind started moaning in a whin bush, we would gulp down the scalding tea offered by our crofter friends and embark in haste with stores and mail-bag. We enjoyed the trip, but it was good to see the water astern widening, and the houses of the island enlarging. And at last the shelter of the home pier, and the welcome crunch of prow on shingle!

Whereas Tanera has a roomy and sheltered anchorage, the opposite shore of Achiltibuie is harbourless and exposed to the south-west, so that even a fresh breeze will raise a sea that makes it hard to launch a small boat in comfort, or to leave her lying in safety. The new pier with its concrete piles, through which waves break and wind sweeps without mercy, was built only for the convenience of steamers: there is no breakwater, no slip for the use and protection of small craft. Boats, especially those roomy enough to carry sheep, are becoming as scarce as the men to handle them; and it looks as if the fine grazing of the Summer Isles, which saves the crippling expense of sending hoggs to be wintered away, will soon be lost for lack of transport.

Yes, it is sad to look at Ardnagoine, and the fertile green strip between houses and shore. Many a fine crop of hay and oats and potatoes must have been raised there once, and might be raised again, for the island is mild, and drier than the mountainous mainland. The houses and byres are still there, in all stages of decay, from nettle-covered heaps of stones and rubble to a cottage with windows and doors, which is now used for a store for hay. A broken skylight lets in rain to rot the wooden floor, and before long this house will follow the rest, and the place be no more than a patch of rough grazing for scrub cattle. It is a pity. For these little isles, from the days of Odysseus and Brendan until now, have led men captive, offering them the completeness of a world within a world, a poor man's kingdom, a solitude fruitful in work and study and contemplation. A desert island is beautiful, because Nature is there alone and unravished. But a deserted island is beautiful only to one who looks at it in the hope and intention of rebuilding.

The evacuation of small islands and of remote parts of the mainland is the last phase of the long Celtic retreat. Beyond that is only the sea, and the isles of the blessed, wherever these may be found. Simple-minded historians talk of extermination when they mean assimilation. Lasting conquests are made less by war than by commerce, and the glamour of an alien civilisation has always been more dangerous than the fire and sword of the invader. An adaptable intelligent people is apt to lose its independence without knowing it, since the delight of running after something new blinds us to its implications. It was not force that brought Manchester slops and cheap newspapers and radio and silk stockings to the remote glens. And yet these things, far more than eviction or penal laws, have destroyed the old self-sufficient culture of the isles, and men's belief in it. Only a complete revaluation can alter that. This may soon be imposed on us by force of circumstances; and one wonders if the new islanders may not be people who have been through civilisation and come out on the other side.

We had no coal on Tanera. Two primus stoves were used for cooking, and the living-room fire was maintained with peat. Most of this was cut from a shallow bank at the back of the house; but in these days the island has been stripped of fuel, and the little that remains is not very good. More was brought in the launch from Eilean a' Chleirich, but six miles of treacherous sea, and the trouble of loading the bags through a heavy surf, made this extra supply rather costly in labour, for a bag of peat does not last long. Indeed the crux of modern peat-winning is transport. The men who first thought of exploiting the bogs had all the world to choose from, and naturally took the easiest and nearest. Their luckless descendants were forced to operate in ever-widening circles, until now, in many places, the hauling takes longer than all the rest of the work. In parts of Ireland, where even townsmen sit round a turf fire, bogs on the very mountain-tops have come into use, and the authorities have built roads to them, so that carts may replace the immemorial traffic of pack asses. To save peat we would often gather driftwood on the beaches of the west and south-west, and bring it round by boat, or carry it across the isle on our backs to the eastern side where we lived.

On any western isle the most interesting shore is that which faces the Atlantic. But few men care to live under so stern a dominion, and those few must have some quality of soul, at once austere and free, that responds to the wildness of their surroundings. Harbours are mostly on the east coast, facing the mainland, and for shelter and ease of transport, houses are built round them. There are other advantages. An east window gets the first light of day, and, as a friend put it, the cheering sight of storm clouds in retreat, rolling exhausted down to leeward. Only in islands with machair land are the chief settlements in the west; a bitter exposure to wind is the price of good ploughland and rich pasture. 'Fast runs the slattern's husband on the machair of Uist',* and a man needs not only sound clothes but a stout heart to make his home on those sand-blown Atlantic plains.

The west side of Tanera has several little bays with pebble beaches, and to the north-west a deep inlet sheltered by a half-tide isle called Eilean Saille. On all these shores there was plenty of driftwood; but in late autumn the sea was rarely calm enough to visit them in the dinghy, and we had to carry our gleanings home by land. The interior of Tanera is a confusion of rocky knolls and boggy hollows scarred with abandoned peat cuttings. In the midst are three freshwater lochans radiating from a point where their heads nearly meet. The pasture is poor enough, for most of the turf was stripped long ago to feed the curer's furnace, and it will take

---

* 'Is luath fear na droch-mhna air a' mhachair Uibhistich.' The suggestion is that if your coat is ragged and buttonless, you must run to keep warm.

many a long year to form again. Sheep will thrive there only if shifted periodically to the rich marine grazings of the small isles. The flocks of Coigeach are mainly Cheviots, brought from the rich pastures of Sutherland, and they soon deteriorate if kept continuously on the Torridonian sandstone.

My first visit to Eilean Saille was on one of those still days in November, with no obvious hint of impending storm, but maybe a 'carry' of high clouds or moan of surf to prove that peace is not offered, but only an armistice. Silence lay over the earth, not broken but emphasised by the continuous roar on the northern ends of the outermost isles and skerries; for some commotion far out on the Atlantic had set a heavy swell rolling in from the stormy wastes beyond the Butt of Lewis. There was a smother of foam on rocks submerged or awash, and arms of spray flung up on the higher ones, so that for all its specious calm, this was no day to land sheep or stores on the smaller isles. In the sheltered bay the sea lay smooth as pewter, and its motion no more than a secret heaving and swinging of seaweed. For it was dead low water at the spring tides, so that trails of tangle were exposed, half floating, half aground, to which the spent turmoil of waves gave the semblance of independent and animal life. Smooth whiplike stems, with curly fronds intact, lay drifting or trailing, while others, snapped off short, reared up like snakes about to strike. There was something obscene and a little frightening in this brief revelation of things normally under water. Waves, groping in sinuous weed, lost force and direction, and their free cry fell to an impotent sighing and hissing, as of strength frustrated and betrayed.

At the edge of the tide a heron stood motionless. Soon he rose with a heavy flap that disguised the speed of his flight. In the deep water beyond the tangle, seals appeared in twos and threes, and looked at me with that penetrating, half-human gaze that explains why so much has been imagined about them. Further up the shore, bladder-wrack lay in orange-tawny heaps, and the dry bladders, together with spume bubbles left by the ebbing tide, exploded in volleys of faint poppings, like fairy artillery. The colour of the seaweed was repeated in the glow of crumbling bracken on the braes. Here and there in sunny hollows, single sprays of pink or purple bell heather still lingered, fair as the bloom they brought to Emily Brontë on the day of her death. Pity, I thought, that she never knew this place. The Yorkshire moors held all her love, as they guard her bones; but she was a Celt on both sides,* and would have found pleasure in the Western Isles she was never allowed to see.

Just before I started on my search for driftwood, we had taken advantage of the exceptionally low tide to lay a new and heavier mooring for the launch. We might then sleep sound on the wildest night, without listening to the wind and wondering if we ought to run down and see if the launch were dragging her anchor. Although it was Sunday, and Achiltibuie lay silent as a city of the dead, our only

---

* Mr Brontë, whose real name was Patrick Prunty, was an Irishman, while Maria Branwell belonged to Penzance. Branwell, a common name in West Cornwall, is probably an anglicised version of Bron whella (highest hill), which appears in a still more garbled form as Brown Willy, the highest point of Bodmin Moor.

neighbour on the isle had consented to give us a hand. Two miles of intervening sea can loosen the ties of custom and, as he once remarked with characteristic shrewdness, he sometimes found it as well to be ignorant of religion.

I carried a length of rope, with a slip-noose at either end. There was driftwood on the south shore of Eilean Saille, and the tide was low enough for me to cross dry-footed. But the ford was slippery with weed lying on round wet stones, and there were pools full of intriguing things that might easily allow the flood to steal a march on my return. So I skirted the inlet, and followed a sheep-track along the western cliffs till I reached a cove called Mul Mor. It held a shelving beach of pebbles the size of antique cannon-balls, and rolls of dead seaweed in parallel rows, marking the limit of each flood tide from lowest neaps to highest springs. Mixed with the seaweed was other wreckage, some cast away by Nature, but more by man: glass balls and corks from nets, bottles of all shapes and sizes, the empty shells of sea-urchins, fragments of sawn timber, branches of trees peeled white by the waves, sections of wooden boxes that once contained margarine or tinned peaches. There were no messages in any of the bottles, a lack which young Alasdair noticed last time we were there, and remedied by setting adrift a blue ribbed bottle, which may once have held Lysol, but now contained a brilliantly inaccurate SOS. Nor were there any of those tropical seeds which the Gulf Stream is said to bring to the western shores of Lewis. The only unusual thing was a damaged but still serviceable creel, and a sheep long in the sea, with bones polished to the semblance of ivory, and wool as white as snow, but draggled, like a tassel of cotton-grass after a night's rain. And among all this harvest of the sea, not a thing that was good to eat, though the U-boats had been busy. 'If a ship must be sunk today,' I thought, 'may it be near Tanera, with a cargo of oranges, bananas, and dates!'

How often in the past, when nearly all those who lived on the shore made their living from the deep, were these lines of wreckage searched for the bodies of sons and lovers. The Gaelic language is rich in terms connected with the sea, having often a single word for what in English must be expressed in periphrasis. This tidal fringe of things cast up can be conveyed by the one word *tiùrr*, as it is in the Hebridean lament for Ailean Donn, who was drowned on the way to his wedding with Anna Campbell in Harris. 'Fain would I go with thee,' she sings, wondering on what shore, among what drifting wrack of the sea he will be washed up, perhaps even in Ireland:

> Ailein Dhuinn, mo ghis is mo ghaire,
> 'S truagh, a Righ, nach mi bha laimh riut,
> Ge b'e eilb no ob an traigh thu,
> Ge b'e tiùrr am fag an làn thu.*

I wandered up and down the shore, looking for anything that might be useful. The creel I fitted with a piece of

* 'Brown Alan, my enchantment and my laughter,
    Pity, O King, I was not near thee,
  On whatever bay or cove of the shore,
    On whatever fringe of the sea the flood tide left thee.'

rope, and filled with small bits of wood for the fire. Next I chose a small bottle to hold methylated spirit for the primus. Larger pieces of wood were bound into a bundle for my back. The green glass balls were not to be resisted; and though I already had several, gathered on the endless sands of South Uist, I put them aside for another time. And even after collecting as much as I could carry, I continued to poke about, speculating on the origin and wanderings of the sheep and of other things that had been long in the sea. In Loch Carron and other landlocked waters I had noticed that old boots and mattresses, and other things easily recognised, would go out with every ebb and come back with every flood, until at last they disintegrated and vanished. But in the open Minch, the drifting stuff I saw might have come from any place at all, and by any route: and should an off-shore squall or an equinoctial tide send it out once more upon its travels, there was little chance that it would ever return to Tanera.

Driftwood, soaked with water and impregnated with salt, is heavy, and even a small load becomes a burden on a rough path. The rope galls, and the bundle slips to an awkward angle. But in following sheep-paths I found the way easier, for the surface of these tracks is packed hard by the treading of countless feet, year after year; and sheep always choose the line of least resistance, and cross burns at the handiest places, so that the most skilful engineer could hardly improve on their work. The slopes above the cove bore many a trace of man's former occupation. Ridges of lazy-beds, made with the primitive crooked spade, will endure for ages after the diggers have gone to dust. On North Rona, abandoned for 250 years, they are still perfect. Indeed, once the ridges are skinned over with turf, and thus protected from erosion, there is nothing to prevent them from lasting indefinitely, since water, gathering and running in the furrows, only increases their depth. In certain slanting lights the old lazy-beds stand out with startling clearness, as do the finer contours of a distant hill.

There was no hurry in the world, except to reach home before it became too dark to find the rough track to the school-house. As I climbed from the beach, the noise of the surf, rising from every shore like a vast breathing, spread and deepened till it seemed to fill the whole earth. And then I found myself singing, with a single frail voice raised like a bird's against the sea's immensity. It was no set song, but an idle drift from one melody to another, becoming at last no tune at all, but an impersonal plaint, like the wind in dry heath-bells, or the shrilling of an oyster-catcher in a cove of the rocks. It is only in listening to natural sounds in their purest form – to the roar of waves or murmur of streams or soughing of pine woods – that one comes to understand the genesis of all folk music, of the airs that have come down to us from the night of ages, when man with his joys and sorrows was not far removed from the wild life around him. Such song requires no instrumental accompaniment, because Nature herself provides it, and that is why, when we hear the sea or the wind, there is so often an irresistible impulse to lift up our voices: an impulse which even in the most sophisticated suburbia drives a man to sing in his bath, from the first gush of the hot tap to the last gurgle of the waste pipe.

When the rope began to cut my shoulder, I slipped off the awkward bundle, and sitting on a stone, took a last look at the day's ending. To the south I could see the promontory of Rudha Re, and away in the south-west the hills of Harris like a cloud-bank on the horizon, and nearer at hand the islands and skerries of the Summer Isles – Eilean a' Chleirich and Glasleac and Stac Mhic Aonghais and many another. Most of the smaller isolated rocks have the same triangular shape, with a long gentle slope to the east, and a short steep one to the west, forming a right angle at the apex, so that they look like beasts sitting to watch the sun go down. Each one of them was fringed with foam, and spray was tossing high on their northern ends. But the open water between was calm, and of an opaque greenish hue, shot here and there with dull metallic gleams. The sky was covered with a pall of high grey cloud, crossed with darker bars and thread-like streamers in rapid motion, heralding wind. Near the horizon were pale slashes of clear sky – loopholes through which a beleaguered world might catch a fleeting glimpse of the light of infinite space.

The tide had turned, covering the beds of weed and the place where the heron had been. Soon it would be dark, with no relief but the intermittent gleam of lighthouses, for the new moon would be set, and the stars hidden in cloud. Fire, and the lamp, and tea set out on the big table, seemed better than the fairest view. I slung up my burden and lifted the creel. The sight of it suggested a second creel, and a

pack-pad between them, and under the pad the broad back
of a pony. Porterage is ever the badge of servitude. Why do
men tame animals, if not to enable themselves to walk like
gods with nothing to carry?

A wealthy country like Britain has room for a large professional and official class, to which men of very diverse origins meet to form a group without land or local tradition. A clever boy leaves his island, his village, his father's house, goes to the university, gets some professional appointment, marries into his new surroundings, and settles down in the city. If he is a Highlander, he will probably return to his native place for holidays and may even dream of retiring there, provided that his wife is willing. His children are brought up as others of the same class, and will look at their origins with distaste, indifference, or perhaps with a kind of impotent nostalgia. The home in which he must rear his family, a villa, or a flat, has indeed more substance than a nomad's tent, but is in a sense less permanent, since it cannot follow his wanderings. A change of work, a rise of salary, and he must abandon it to another – itself and the garden he carefully made in leisure hours. It is too temporary, too impersonal to shelter any pieties or to gather a tradition. The household gods cannot keep themselves warm at a gas fire.

And so the young people of the professional classes, having little to keep them at home, push out willingly to something new, perhaps abroad. Free from the ties of tradition, it is all the easier for them to make fine seamen, bold adventurers, adaptable colonists. I often think that the old Norsemen must have had shallow roots, like the pines that grow in the thin soil of their own mountains. Their wooden houses were readily exchanged for the ships that served them better and earned their deeper love. On land they never had a great foothold. In the Western Isles, after an occupation lasting nearly 400 years, they left nothing behind but many names of places, a few names of persons, and a number of loan words in Gaelic, mostly connected with ships and the sea.

And when the time comes for these rovers to retire, it will not be to the casual peripatetic home of their youth, but to some place in tune with their personal tastes and desires. Highlanders are notoriously home-loving; but when I asked the captain of a liner, then on his last voyage, if he meant to return to his native Lewis, he replied that he had bought a house outside Sydney. 'I've spent forty years in tropical seas,' he said, 'and I want the sun.' Some of us also want the sun, or what it symbolises, and go to seek it in a strange country. There we may find congenial work, pleasant companions, beautiful surroundings, even the sense of inner fitness and harmony that is the fruit of spiritual contentment. But we must pay for it. We start without a past, without sponsors: we have all to make for ourselves. As Chaucer tersely puts it, 'Thou knittest thee where thou art not received, And where thou wouldest be, thence art thou waved'. Years pass before we are accepted into our chosen community, if ever we are; and even if we pass the first barrier, there will always be something alien about us, so that in the most intimate gatherings we shall find no place, and when we enter a sudden silence will fall. In a moment of strong emotion, and to someone dearly loved, it is easy to say, 'Thy people shall be my people, and thy God my God'. But to accept its implication day by day, without intimacy, is another story. Even the Moabite woman, with her youth and beauty, brought into the land by one native and destined to marry another, must have had her lonely bitter hours. 'Why have I found grace in thine eyes, that thou shouldest take knowledge of me, seeing that I am a stranger?'

The British people have always shown kindness and hospitality to foreigners and refugees of all sorts, even to the extent of admitting that the best English prose of the present century was written by a Pole. No one will ever know what spiritual impulse made Conrad adopt our language and customs; there is nothing distinctively British about him except perhaps his knowledge of the sea and of the souls of seamen. His temper and outlook are those of the creative artist of any age or land. If he chose to write in a language not his own, he is only following the example of many Slavs who wished to be known outside their own country. But he is alone in doing it better than the natives – a thing much easier to understand when we remember how, in Lord Jim and Captain Whalley and old Singleton, he was able to reach the heart of the most reticent race on earth.

Ireland has always been passionately loved. Nowhere else has patriotism, that uncomfortable virtue that so often wavers between smug complacency and hysterical chauvinism, risen to higher levels of poetry and devotion. For

Ireland is poor, unfortunate, beautiful, unmanageable – the very qualities to inspire a love that does not count the cost. An empire on which the sun never sets could not be praised in the language of Cathleen na Houlihan or of the Dark Rosaleen. It was Columcille, so many centuries ago, who said, 'My heart is broken within my breast: if death comes to me soon, it will be because of the great love I bear to the Gael.' He worked and died in another land, but he was an Irishman, and 'the grey eye' that looked back on Ireland was as Irish as those of a million emigrants watching the Tearaght light drop below the eastern horizon. There is a little hill in Iona which still bears the name Cul ri Eirinn (back turned to Ireland), for, according to tradition, the saint was determined not to settle till he lost sight of his native land, and this was the first isle from which the Irish coast was no longer visible.

What is even more remarkable about Ireland is the spell she puts on the outsider, and not for the sake of any wealth or comfort he will find there. Alien settlers have become more Irish than the Irish themselves (*Hiberniores Hibernis*) and many of the keenest patriots have been of foreign or of half-foreign extraction. The charm of Ireland is very hard to explain, and its strength can only be realised on Irish soil, and more especially in the west. For here we reach the last outpost of European race and culture, or as the Hebrideans have said of their own islands, 'the true edge of the great world' (*Fior iomall an domhain mhoir*). If you cannot love Ireland, you must hate her, for there is no middle way in a land that runs altogether to extremes and anomalies. Here is the only neutral member of the British Commonwealth at war, the only state with a modern constitution explicitly based on Christianity, the only country with an official language that hardly anyone speaks at home. The fruits of Irish learning and missionary enterprise were once spread over the whole of north-western Europe. The treasures of Irish art, both pagan and Christian – things like the Tara brooch and the *Book of Kells* – are unequalled in their kind. Yet, just a hundred years ago, two centuries of abject misery culminated in the great potato famine, when the countrymen of saints and scholars lay dying like flies at the roadside, and no one cared. Compared with what happened in Ireland from the days of Cromwell to those of Parnell, the sufferings of the Scottish Gaels, even in the Sutherland clearances and the Lochboisdale deportations, are nothing. We may blame this person or that institution, and point to a picture of constant misgovernment and misunderstanding. The Englishman, they say, good-natured and well-meaning as he is, can never understand the Irish temperament. But I am wondering if they can understand it themselves, strange and elusive as it is: and still more if a land so bewitched can be governed at all. Can you hold the wind in a net, or plumb the bottomless bog with a stick?

It is not merely the beauty of scenery and atmosphere, the farmer's lure of grass that is green all winter, that gives Ireland its unique charm. There are green pastures in New Zealand, and mountains and sea in the Highlands. But Ireland has a quality of enchantment that is not to be found in Scotland, except perhaps in the Western Isles. You come, and there is no reason why you should ever go away. The claims of family, business, country, dwindle to a pin-point; you have found your place, and there you stay. One evening in November, on the western side of Valentia Island, I saw a ragged-looking fellow stalking rabbits with a gun. I gave him a greeting, and was answered in a rich East Anglian accent. We fell into conversation, and he told me that he was an Essex farmer's son who had gone wandering in the world; and one day, finding himself in London with empty pockets, he met a young man he had once befriended. This young man's aunt had just died, leaving him enough to live on; and he proposed that the two should go to Kerry, which he knew, for a little shooting. They went. 'That was five years ago,' he concluded. 'We have often thought of coming away, but somehow we never did, and now I suppose we never shall.' How easily might the same happen to any one of us in such a place!

And most easily to myself. For I have always loved Ireland, years before I ever set foot in it. When Terence MacSwiney, Mayor of Cork, starved himself to death in Lincoln Jail, I was a very young lecturer at an English university. My colleagues laughed at him, and I lost my temper, and went away somewhere to cry with rage. They were right to laugh; viewed from an English common-room, it was all fantastic. Only I was looking at it from the other side of the water; and when, many years later, I went to Ireland, it was like entering a country often seen in dreams, familiar and more than familiar – profoundly part of yourself, but in another dimension. I have always hated newspapers, but I found myself reading the *Irish Independent* and the *Cork Examiner* from cover to cover, like any old clubman with his *Times*. These papers were racy, homely, with more space given to local interests than to the affairs of the great world.* I have always hated politics; but in Ireland they have a fatal attraction. For public life in a small country, where everyone knows everyone and the issues are mainly domestic, is much as it was in the old city state: indifference is impossible. In Solon's Athens people were fined for not joining a political party. In Ireland this would be unnecessary. To take sides, even to the length of prejudice and intolerance, is in the air; and you cannot avoid it, even if you wish. And somehow you don't wish.

When I visited the National Museum in Dublin, an Irish friend told me to be sure not to miss the 1916 Room. It is a curious exhibition, consisting mainly of moth-eaten Republican uniforms, cloth caps with bullet holes, and faded letters from men awaiting execution. I remember a coarse china cup, of the kind provided in railway buffets, from which Padraig Pearse drank the last tea he would get on earth. Viewed from this side of the Irish Sea, the 1916 Room, like MacSwiney's hunger strike, may seem fantastic, even childish: but over there it is a matter for pride, perhaps for tears; at any rate it is real, as a university common-room is not. I came out of the 1916 Room with the feeling that I understood many things that before had seemed inexplicable. For all her antiquity, her traditions, her tragic and glorious past, Ireland, like the Western Isles, has discovered the secret of eternal youth. It

---

* There was much ado about the extravagance and threatened insolvency of the Kerry County Council, and about a man who refused to pay his rates, because the demand note was not presented in Irish.

is as if the blood and tears that have been shed on Irish soil were part of a struggle towards a new and splendid experiment in living. There is a well-known prophecy about Iona, attributed to Columcille, which I cannot refrain from quoting once more:

> An I mo chridhe, I mo ghraidh,
>   An aite guth mhanach bidh geum ba;
> Ach mu'n tig an saoghal gu crich,
>   Bidh I mar a bha.*

Behind Iona stands Ireland; and it is possible that Europe may again find spiritual and intellectual light in the farthest and poorest isles of the west.

Ireland is still, as she has always been, the hearth-stone of the Gael, and if she goes down, farewell to any important survival of Gaelic culture. Just as the Highland literary revival has lagged far behind its Irish counterpart, so the prospects of an effective Scottish nationalism are not very hopeful. If the 1916 Rebellion opened a chapter of history, the defeat at Culloden very definitely brought one to a close. Since the Union, the Scottish Gaels have advanced by slow and Parliamentary stages, through the Crofters' Act and the housing subsidies, into the promised land of southern prosperity and uniformity, with a few songs and pibrochs

---

*   'In Iona of my love,
        Instead of monks' voice shall be lowing of cows.
      But before the world comes to an end
        Iona shall be as it was.'

to enliven the inevitable dullness. As an attempt to achieve a much-needed decentralisation, or as a means of preserving local custom and tradition, the Scottish nationalist movement has its place: but a living political force it can never be. The average Scot – and it must be remembered that the majority of Scotsmen are not Highland – sees that the Union pays. Bred in a harder climate, and of a rather different racial stock, he is shrewder and more practical than the Irishman, and his memory for the old unhappy things far less tenacious. If there are good jobs to be had in England or in the Dominions, whereby personal and national dignity can be upheld, then never mind about Wallace and Bruce and a Parliament in Edinburgh. These things are shadows, well enough for a Burns' night but not common sense. No Scot in authority would compel county councillors to wear the kilt, or have the Glasgow tram tickets printed in Gaelic. Perhaps it is a loss, for in these days of devastating uniformity, anything individual, however freakish, is to be welcomed with open arms. But it is not common sense.

I seem to have wandered far from my starting point, and someone may be getting angry. But it is the habit of wayfaring men to wander to and fro, and I who have found contentment far from the land of my birth, shall never be other than a stranger. Born in a city and reared in a garden so narrow that balls and arrows going out of bounds would be found two doors away, I can't remember the time when I did not long for the wilderness. Now I have it, thank God, and shall keep it to the end, taking my *strubag* at the hospitable hearth, and going out again into the night. 'I was lonesome all times,' says Christy Mahon in the *Playboy*, 'and was born lonesome, I'm thinking, as the moon of dawn.'

But such is the life of man.

'Pity you were not here in summer!' How often have I heard that phrase repeated, till I feel like knocking down the next person who says it. It is as if your old friend were for ever regretting that you could not see him in his best clothes. For just as he looks most natural, most friendly in his worn tweeds and spattered boots, with maybe a splash of mud on his nose, so a beloved place will reveal its truth in winter, when people have time for a crack on the road or at the door, and the fall of the leaf discloses the rarer colours, and the naked shapes of hills and trees without excess of vegetation, without midges and clegs, without the restlessness of strangers and the drone of the cars they ride in. There is a shy and haunting charm in winter, as there is in the wrinkled face of an old seaman, when eyes under shaggy brows light up with a rare slow smile.

To many of us the thought of a peat moss in November is altogether abominable. It is a vision of stark desolation, of gloom without end, an unwarranted assault upon our order and security by the ancient powers we thought long since subdued. Those who have seen all unprepared, from the train that skirts it, the Moor of Rannoch at dusk and in storm, might easily think it the antechamber of some northern Avernus, a place of penance for souls who had loved too much the lighted shop windows:

To Whinny Muir thou com'st at last,
And Christ receive thy saule!

A desert brimming with water, oozy with mud and moss, without trees save those embedded in centuries of peat, formless, shelterless, ungrazed, gashed with the peat-knife and rutted with ancient cart-tracks: this is no place to linger in. Let us get home, and turn on all the lights. November too is abominable, a Cinderella of months, associated by townsmen with the creeping fog of valleys tainted with smoke and contracting daylight, and stealthy cold reaching out from late dawn till early dusk, and the slow death of all things with never a hint of spring.

The countryman has a wider vision, a sturdier faith. For him November is a month of fruition, rich with the promise of comfort, with the dawn of leisure. His fields are cleared, his barns full and battened down to endure the gales and frost of winter. He has time now to enjoy his home, to potter about with a gun; and this pottering, apparently so aimless, may end in rabbits or snipe or woodcock, providing a dinner and satisfying the ancient lust of the chase. And not only that, but some unacknowledged longing for space and freedom and beauty will also be satisfied – a desire for which he has his own understatements: 'Time to do what I like . . . room to swing a cat' and other phrases designed to express, and at the same time to conceal, an emotion that seems silly or extravagant in words. He would be ashamed to walk for walking's sake; that would be 'mooning', and make him feel awkward, like kisses at a railway station. He knows that the earth is asleep, not dead, and can find a promise of spring in things that still linger – green grass under a sheltered dyke, a tuft of defiant yellow ragwort, a spray of cranesbill with delicate pink flowers and spiked seed-vessel, under the shade of a rock beside the burn.

When I go out to the moss in November, it is not to call up the ghost of summer, as a lover might study the face of his ageing mistress in a vain attempt to recapture a vanished past. I can see it still, and know it will come again: the waving plumes of the cottongrass, the rich hot smell of sun-smitten earth, bog pools warm to the feet, the song of larks and murmur of bees, the droning talk of peat-cutters, blue smoke curling from pipes and from under kettles of tea. I can see it still, and nothing is fairer. But what is before me now has a charm subtler, quieter, and far more intimate. If you love the moss in November, then be sure that the wild has yielded you some part of its secret, and henceforward you will be no longer a stranger.

There are places in the Highlands where mountain walls recede, leaving wide tracts of level ground, solitary, treeless, seamed with the stony beds of shallow rivers, and here and there a lonely lochan, not gloomy like a tarn among the hills, but pensive and withdrawn, as if it were always twilight on its shores. On the verge of these mosses you may see a few white homesteads, flanked by cornstacks; but peat-land rarely repays drainage, and where husbandry has dared to encroach, it is met with stubborn resistance. Over a frontier zone of mossy grazing, abandoned to rushes and rabbits, is waged the truceless war of the wild with the sown, where man's strength is worn down by subtle opposition, and his energy sapped by the easy fatalism of the nomad. These places, from early June to the end of September, yield summer grazing, but they are dangerous with bogs and holes and their most valuable product is fuel. You cannot go far without seeing a freshly cut bank, with water at its foot – water whose black bottom makes it reflect, as no other medium can, the changing face of the sky: and beside it, massive stacks, well-fenced from cattle, standing on ground already deep with the dust of their predecessors.

At one time, when staying in Argyll, I used to walk every evening from about an hour before sunset till dark, and my track was as monotonous as a professor's constitutional. Not indeed because there was no other possible walk, but because I like to go west at sundown, especially if I am anywhere near the sea. The road was straight and level with moors on either hand. On the right was one of those lochans I have spoken of, with a clump of Scots firs on its shore. These black and secret trees, last survivors of the old Caledonian forest, had, like all doomed creatures, a grim and furtive look, and in that twilight hour seemed to have gathered their own premature night. To the right was another bog, bounded by a range of low grassy hillocks, with sprawling, contorted whin bushes upon them. These hillocks, and some rising ground beyond, concealed the long-drawn waters of Loch Linnhe, so that this moss, like the Moor of Rannoch, seemed to stretch to the very foot of the distant hills. The wide levels of standing water, the spaced hills, gave to the place a look of Ireland. If this was Deirdre's adopted country, 'dear land of the east', no wonder she felt at home in it. The very name of Argyll – Earraghaidheil means East Gaels – must have been given by people looking at it from the west – and whence more likely than from Ireland? There were open gates at points along the road leading to looming stacks of peat. Sheep were picking among the withered bent, with amber eyes glancing from smooth black faces, to which the curved horns gave a keen intelligent look. At the roadside were some crossbred stirks of an Ayrshire type whose breath was like faint smoke in the chilly air.

There had been heavy rain not long before, but the sky was breaking behind Mull, so that a wild gleam fell on chains of glimmering puddles down the road, and on drops strung like beads on wires of a fence. Grey-black clouds rolled east to dissolve in sheets of rain on the hills round Ballachulish. Among the heights of Appin the rain had ceased, and wisps of mist floated motionless against the purple slopes, with here and there a coppery glow where some wandering beam fell upon withered bracken. But even the richness of these colours paled before the tawny orange and russet glory of the bent and the tussock grass at my feet – a colour marvellous in itself, and intensified by the wetness of earth and air. Its fiery glow, its incredible depth, was enhanced by the blackness of peat stacks, the gloomy purple of the hills, the ghostly sheen of pools and the whiteness of spume balls quivering at the mouth of a running drain.

I was looking at all that, and wondering how anyone could find dullness in November, or depression in a moss like this, when I heard the grinding of wheels on the gravelly road, and saw an oldish man leading a horse and cart with a load of peats. He was going my way, so I fell in beside him and we began a conversation, rather loud and disjointed, for the cart was making a good deal of noise. He asked me where I came from, and when I replied from Ross-shire, he said, 'That's very far away in the north . . . wasn't it somewhere near you that Walter Elliot – you mind he was Secretary for Scotland – lost his wife climbing in the hills? . . . Is it wild with woods where you come from?' And then we fell to talking of other distant places, and with the wistful longing so often heard in Highland voices when speaking of the golden south, he told me about a relative 'who went to the Salisbury Plains and became quite Englified. . . . That's the country to farm in. There's nothing here – it rains all the time.' I suggested that at the present time 'the Salisbury Plains' would be wild with bombs and barbed wire, which might be worse for farming than woods or even the rain itself. But I don't think he believed me. It is a fine thing to be able to find the land of heart's desire on a map of the British Isles, and have nothing to do but look up trains and buy a ticket. Only you must never go further than that, or the vision will recede and your self be standing disconsolate in some place not nearly as good as the one you left.

After a while he wished me good night and turned through a gate leading to the shore. I went a little further, with the lonesome sound of retreating wheels in my ear, till the road ended in a bridge marked 'Private', which gave access to a small island covered with trees. Among these trees was a mansion-house – or so I was told, for I never set eyes on it. The strait was no wider than the Cherwell at Magdalen Bridge, and it was now the time of unusually high spring tides. There was still an hour or so to go before high water, and the tide was flowing under the bridge at eight knots or more, swirling and eddying like a river in spate, and piling against the central piers of the bridge in glassy green curves, which gave the illusion of rapids on a sloping river-bed. Above the bridge, where the channel was wider and the tide less strong, a few adventurous ducks were trying to breast the current in midstream; but finding themselves drifting ever nearer to the rushing narrows, they made for the quieter waters inshore. The close of the day was windless and profoundly still. I heard nothing but the gurgle and hiss of the streaming tide, and from time to time a sighing along the shore, as one of those smooth mysterious wells that visit sea lochs, even in the calmest weather, broke on the shingle below.

The ugly pretentious ironwork of the modern bridge could not destroy the haunting charm of this island, which is called Eriska. The Norsemen have left their mark on all the western seaboard of Scotland, and this name, like the Hebridean Eriskay, means Eric's Isle. That Eric, whoever he may have been, had a fine taste in islands, whether bare to the sky or mysteriously wooded. 'Is it wild with woods where you come from?' Even here, in the gentler land of Argyll, the woods seem wild enough, when seen motionless under brooding clouds and guarded by tides that run like a mill race. I saw the place again at low water, when the strait was a weed-fringed trickle, and under brighter skies, but my first impression remained unchanged.

Turning home, I noticed a grassy spit of land, about a mile away to the south-west, and upon it a little group of farm buildings, shadowed by two or three tall and leafless trees. A friendly place, with the tide brimming up to the grass of the steading.

Presently I came to a substantial farmhouse and buildings, surrounded by the ash and beech trees that give grace and shelter to many a steading in Lorne. The place was full of the familiar noises of evening, to which the swift November dusk had given a deeper significance, as if we were hearing them from the world's edge, and for the last time. Cattle gathered by dogs from a marshy field came clumsily splashing, urged by the shrill cries of a woman with a long stick, till they reached the road and filed quietly into the steading. Stirks at the awkward age between weaning and the second spring, with rough coats and dirty flanks, were trailing along the muddy lane, driven by an oldish man with a sou'wester drawn down over placid brows. From somewhere within came a joyous quacking of ducks, rising in crescendo as if a speech were being applauded: the grunt of a questing pig, the wistful moan of a housed bull, the clatter of pails, voices, barking – all the evening traffic of a farm, so often repeated yet never quite the same. And then a drift of peat smoke, holding in its fugitive scent the whole delight of coming in from the field at the end of day. Night is the best herdsman, bringing home man and beast, as all pastoral people know, Greeks and Gaels alike. There would be flames dancing on the ceiling, the steady glow of lamplight, a table spread, dogs sleeping on the hearth, a smell of baking, perhaps of fried herring. And at the table, people who smile in welcome, and the memory of faces no longer there: faces that look on alien skies in this world or some other; and for the loneliest of us, faces that never smiled but in our heart's desire. All this and more. The memories of a thousand years that are as yesterday are held in that enchanting smell, from the camp fires of the first wanderers on earth to the kitchen reek of Ballure, sniffed by a passing traveller on the road and never forgotten.

Now there is nothing easier to sentimentalise than the smell of peat smoke. 'Peat!' they exclaim. 'How marvellous! Do you really burn it at home?' And they forget, if they ever knew, the weariness, the precarious cutting and saving of the stuff, the hopeless rapidity with which it burns away, the dust it leaves in the room, especially among books. And yet this facile sentiment, like so many others, harbours a truth, solid as the fact at the heart of the most extravagant romance. So that the person who starts to debunk peat smoke, as I often feel like doing, and sometimes actually do if there is some gushing listener to shock, is mainly intent on hiding his own profound if sneaking affection for the thing to be debunked. You hate to see your heart's love smeared over with treacle: get sandpaper then, and rub as hard as you can.

By now the sun had set, and the russet and black of the moss was fading into the mists of night. A mournful wind arose, humming in the telegraph wires and in the strands of the wayside fence, as it would be humming in the rigging of ships at anchor. To those who live on the coast, the noise of wind in wires must always suggest the coming of night at sea, with the broken glimmer of wave-crests under the stars. The sprawling whin bushes took on shapes contorted and terrifying, like beasts crouching to spring. There was a whirr of unseen wings, a gurgle of unseen water. Somewhere in those empty spaces, both on that night and many others, I heard whistling fresh and clear, though no living creature ever appeared.

Not far off was a *sithean* or fairy mound, covered with a thicket of hazel and birch. My landlady, who belonged to a family of teachers, and had been reared in Aberdeen, was anxious to find out if I, coming as I did from a place far off and wild with woods, might perhaps cherish a belief in fairies, waterhorses, and second sight. Now I have lived too long on the far side of the Border to give anything away, and can hardly understand myself, still less explain to another, those modern theories of time that have made second sight a phenomenon respected by professors. So I hid behind that useful Highland formula 'I couldn't say indeed', and had not the courage to tell her that I had given up a good teaching job to dawdle after cows and cut peats in the wet and unprofitable west.

There is a little Gaelic grammar – and an excellent one it is – which proudly proclaims on its cover how many thousands of copies have been sold. Yes, sold, and no doubt studied, and perhaps inwardly digested. And then . . . ? As Hell is paved with good intentions, so are the Highlands strewn with handbooks thrown away by people who began to learn Gaelic and gave it up in despair. The reason is not far to seek. It is not so much the stupidity or impatience of learners, or the difficulty of the language itself, as the unfavourable conditions under which it must be learned. Not that I am pretending that Gaelic is easy. The structure and vocabulary of a Celtic language have very little in common with English. Yet I should not call it harder than French: indeed in some ways it is much easier. Who has not wept over French irregular verbs? Yet in Gaelic there are only ten of these pests, and they can be mastered in a week. And the rest of the grammar, though declensions in decadence can give you many a sly stab in the back, is not really formidable. Nor need we English speakers, with our fantastic spelling, grumble at Gaelic orthography. It is true that the language is horribly difficult to pronounce, so that no one who has not learned it in childhood can hope to speak it with a tolerable accent. But patience and perseverance may give us one no viler than that with which we excruciate the ears of our neighbours across the Channel.

What then is the root of the difficulty? It is the Gael's perfect mastery of English. In theory, a common language should be a help, but in practice, except at the beginning, it is the devil and all. Even in the islands, everyone, except a few very old people, has excellent and copious English, learned from the age of five when first attending school.* Most of them have at one time or other been at work on the mainland or in English-speaking ships. In Barra I have heard people who never left home, and never use English at all but to some chance visitor or official, speak with an elegance and correctness that puts the slipshod Southerner to shame. Why then, in the name of courtesy and common sense, should they suffer you to blunder along in slow and halting Gaelic, when you could be enjoying a reasonable and interesting conversation in English? And on your side, will you not feel ashamed of boring your kind and intelligent friends, and torturing their ears with your crude and cacophonous noises?

Some of the younger people who have been away to town affect to despise the Gaelic, but this attitude is less common

* There is nothing in the Highlands corresponding to the 'Kiltartan English' of the Anglo-Irish drama. The Scottish Gael's English is the correct book language as learned in school and from reading. It may contain a Gaelic idiom or two, and the native Gaelic speaker betrays himself by his treatment of English sounds not heard in Gaelic, like *th* which is frequently pronounced *s*, and long *i* and short *u*, which are assimilated to Gaelic *ao* or *aoi*, as well as by the aspiration so often heard before final *t* or *ck*.

in the islands, where the shooting lodge and all it stands for have less influence, or as in Barra, does not exist at all. In any case the learner must be prepared to be thought an eccentric dabbler whose capers may be politely humoured but not taken seriously. This point of view was expressed with exquisite tact and terseness by a Barra woman to whom I remarked (in Gaelic) that my dog was too old to learn a strange language. 'Wise dog,' she replied in English, not intended for the dog alone. A few, a very few enthusiasts will help you along the stony path, even up to the point of correcting your mistakes. But most of them think, and no doubt they are right – that you are wasting your time and theirs; and this atmosphere, unless you are prepared to discount it and plod along in lonely persistence, is apt to kill with discouragement. Your only hope is to live with an elderly couple in a remote place, and even there you won't get away from the English. It would take much intelligence and more persistence to acquire good French or German under similar conditions.

What after all does it matter? 'Three fair things,' says a Gaelic triad: 'a tree in bloom, a ship under sail, and a holy man on his death bed.'* In our own day we have seen the ship under sail, the fairest thing ever made by man, vanish from the seas of the world. The tree in bloom is still there, but the holy man's death bed is shared by the language he spoke. For no one with any knowledge of history can deny that Gaelic is doomed. Rhetorical questions expect no answer,

* 'Craobh fo bhlàth, long fo sheòl, agus duine naomh air leabaidh a bhàis.'

but if the writer of *Am Faigh a' Ghàidhlig bàs?** is seeking for information, the reply, as the Government official would say, is in the affirmative. The only thing that remains uncertain is when. Every census reveals fewer Gaelic speakers. In the islands, where the children still speak the old language out of school, and external influences count for less, Gaelic may well persist for several more generations. For here it seems to have survived the first shock of modernisation, and has settled down amicably beside official English, as a shrewd old countryman might share his seat with a smart young man from town. But on the mainland, where except in remote corners, hardly a word is commonly heard on the lips of the young, I doubt if it can last more than another generation, unless its life is artifically prolonged. Mainland Gaelic is full of English words, and you will often hear speakers jump from one language to the other with more dexterity than elegance, in the same conversation, or even in the same sentence.

Gaelic must die: and its death will bring to a close a long and splendid tradition. It might be that if the Irish language movement were to succeed in any striking and permanent fashion, there would be some answering stir in Scotland. But there is not much hope.

According to the experts, the Gaelic sound system is the most elaborate in Europe – a thing which the unhappy learner, wandering forlorn among mazy diphthongs and triphthongs, will never wish to dispute. And Gaelic poetry,

---

* 'Shall Gaelic die?' A popular modern song.

with its complicated internal assonances, comes nearest to rendering in speech the values of pure music. This is one reason why translations from Gaelic are often so unsatisfactory. I have always hated Macpherson's *Ossian*, and Mrs. Kennedy Fraser's English versions – translations they are not – of the songs of the Hebrides. There is about them something woolly, sentimental, unreal, which is never found in the original. For in losing the language we lose the music; it is rather as if we went to hear a Beethoven sonata, and instead were given a lecture about it. The best way of translating Gaelic poetry into English is to give a fairly literal rendering into simple prose, as was done by Carmichael in *Carmina Gadelica*.

This closeness to the form of music helps to explain two defects of Gaelic poetry – its prolixity, and its tendency to put sound before sense, and the decoration before the book. As the text of the *Book of Kells* is lost in the manifold magnificence of its margins, so the matter of many a poem is drowned in the spate of its eloquence. Not a few of them are long – much too long. In most the loss of a line, or even of a stanza or two, would not spoil the whole. Gaelic folksongs, even those intended for repetitive labour, have far more verses than English ones: put a Highland *oran luadhaidh* beside an English sea shanty – though perhaps it is unfair to compare men's eloquence with women's!

If you want to translate an English poem into Gaelic, and keep the same number of lines, these lines must be much longer. There is a definite lack of terseness, though the language is perfectly capable of it. As for the subordination of sense to music, or of matter to manner, this criticism sounds worse than it really is. It does not mean that Gaelic poetry has any of the vague, woolly mysticism that grows so readily in suburban soil. The Highlander's vision is direct, concrete; he sees and praises the visible beauty of Nature round him, and his sorrow is no dim *Weltschmerz*, but the human pain of loss, poverty, and exile. Yet the thought, sharp and clear as it is, is often fragmentary, with the beauty of racing cloud or breaking seas. It is significant that the Celts have produced no formal drama, and the old epic poems consist of episodes loosely strung together.

For literary purposes Gaelic has one great advantage – its freedom from debasing associations. Words, like any other thing in constant use, are bound to become not only linguistically worn down, but stamped with the impress of the minds that use them. The vocabulary of a widely spread language like French or English, ranging from the highest poetry to the lowest slang of the slums, must of necessity gather associations from which it is hard to set it free. But Gaelic is the language of a small homogeneous community, unvulgarised, unmechanised. Whatever his other faults, the Scottish Gael is never vulgar, low, or foul-mouthed.* To him Gaelic is the language of religion, of the affections, of the home. It has an intimacy, a solemnity possessed by no other. It is the natural expression of people reared for generations in a land which is not only one of the world's most beautiful, but in some way especially near to the heart.

---

* There are plenty of Gaelic oaths, but to be really offensive you must swear in English.

'If there's ever any misfortune coming to this world,' says Bartley Fallon, 'it's on myself it pitches, like a flock of crows on seed potatoes.'* The same might be said of the Celtic languages. Instead of being allowed to die in decent privacy and quiet, down swoop the philologists and the mystics to see what they can find. Scholars of all nations, attracted by an ancient culture hardly touched by Rome, have come flocking in scores, especially to the study of Irish. No one would grudge this excellent work, did it not give to the general public an impression that these languages are no more than a heap of dry bones, without living interest. On the other hand, the beauty of the west, its peace, its antiquity, have attracted a host of people wishing to satisfy those vague yearnings which are a common symptom of our revolt against the machine. But the thing they want is not where they seek it. As an ancient Irish quatrain says of pilgrimages:

> To go to Rome,
> Much trouble, little profit.
> The King you seek you will not find
> Unless you bring him with you.

They have brought much wealth to steamship companies, and the phrases of Fiona Macleod have now found their way into folders for tourists, where let them rest.

It is a sad thing that Gaelic should die, with so much of its wealth of beauty and richness untouched. For the Highland

* Lady Gregory, Spreading the News.

writer who wishes not merely to make money but to find a wide public must write in English. Now as English is my native tongue, and as I have spent much time and thought in trying to write it well, I am going to allow myself a little rope. It is not easy to write good English, for you must be forever steering a course between the dull monosyllables of common speech and the Latin verbiage of Government officials. Our Saxon forefathers were rude enough, in truth, and it is their doing that some of the most solemn words in our language – God, church, dead, speech, to mention a few that occur to me – should also be some of the ugliest. Where would Milton and Keats have been without our Latin and Norman–French loan words? And yet no one would wish to write like a Blue Book. The loss of inflexions, however much time it saves, robs a language of its variety and some of its charm. Anyone who has tried to write harmonious English will be pestered at every step by the inordinate number of *s*'s he encounters – whole hissing nests of snakes at every step – due in great part to our using this graceless letter to form possessives and plurals; and as if that were not enough, half our *c*'s are reduced to this barbaric sound. In this matter Gaelic is wiser. *c* is always hard; genitives and plurals do not sibilate; *s* in contact with *e* or *i* is pronounced *sh*; and every *s* when aspirated (which only too often occurs) has the value of *h*. I should like to add that although there are a great many *s*'s in this paragraph, I did not introduce them of set purpose, but just took them as they came.

Ages ago Gaelic was doomed, perhaps even before St Margaret drove it from the court of Scotland. And its decline, though hastened by pressure from without, was caused by neglect from within. If by some miracle it should survive, it will be in the Islands, where an autonomous culture might conceivably be formed. And in its death, it will have good company, for many stout souls of heroes have gone down into the shadows. As long as hills stand fast and rivers run, the beautiful place-names will endure, recalling the days that are gone, like Avon and Severn among the newer fields and towns of the south.

December is wild and dark in the Western Isles. But at the second Christmas of the war, as if Nature were offering the truce rejected by men, came a few days of calm clear weather, when Barra slept on the breast of a sea without guile and disarmed. I had been at ceilidh till near midnight, and feeling disinclined for bed, I walked about on the machair of Allasdale until far into the small hours. The sheen of a thousand stars, reflected in rock pools and in wet sand, and a deep auroral glow in the north-west gave light enough to see the sweeping curves of the dunes, and the long white line, hissing and faintly luminous, that divided sea from land. There was no wind to stir the bent-grass at my feet, no swell to heave the unwrinkled face of the waters, which sighed and crooned along the whole length of the isle; and so gentle was this movement, that the breaking of individual waves on rocks or on sand could be clearly distinguished.

It is on nights like this, rather than in the crash and confusion of storm, that we realise the sea's immensity, its strength, and its abysmal treachery. The shores of Barra, so lovingly caressed, were strewn with planks and pit-props and broken lifeboats; and now and again a body would come with the flood, and lie stranded among the tangle and jetsam of the deep. For this pitiful wreckage, cast on the waters by the greed and hatred of men, we cannot blame the sea. Yet it shows no atoning mercy. The seaman, faithful to duty, who loses his ship in storm of battle, will get no better treatment than he who betrays it by his own negligence or folly. The rain falls on the just and the unjust alike, and the sea is equally impartial, equally heartless.

A sailor may honour his calling and love his ship, but is under no illusions about the sea. It may give him a living, and satisfy his lust for adventure; it will test his courage, demand every ounce of his strength, and then as likely as not will take the ship of his love, and his life as well. Conrad, who combined the practical seaman's wisdom with the insight of an imaginative artist, had learned this lesson, and does not let us forget it. 'The sea has never been friendly to man. . . . As if it were too great, too mighty for common virtues, the ocean has no compassion, no faith, no law, no memory. Its fickleness is to be held true to man's purposes only by an undaunted resolution and by a sleepless, armed, jealous vigilance, in which perhaps there has always been more hate than love. . . . The most amazing wonder of the deep is its unfathomable cruelty.'[*]

The following chapter contains one of the grimmest and most moving stories ever told of the sea. As a junior officer, Conrad was sent to rescue the crew of a Danish brig drifting waterlogged and dismasted in mid-Atlantic. It was one of those days of hazy sunshine when the whole world seems asleep. The brig when sighted was slowly settling, and the

---

[*] *The Mirror of the Sea*, chapters 35 and 36.

men, dazed with hunger and fatigue, were still labouring at the pumps. As the rescuing boat drew near, 'the scuppers of the brig gurgled softly all together when the water, rising against her sides, subsided sleepily with a low wash, as if playing about an immovable rock. Her bulwarks were gone fore and aft, and one saw her bare deck low-lying like a raft, and swept clear of boats, spars, houses – of everything except the ring-bolts and the heads of the pumps. I had a dismal glimpse of it as I braced myself up to receive upon my breast the last man to leave her – the captain, who literally let himself fall into my arms.'

Before his rescuers had time to reach their own ship, they saw the brig go down. 'The run of the slight swell was so smooth that it resembled the undulation of a piece of shimmering grey silk shot with gleams of green. . . . For a moment the succession of silky undulations ran on innocently. I saw each of them swell up the misty line of the horizon, far, far away beyond the derelict brig, and the next moment, with a slight friendly toss of our boat, it had passed under us and was gone. . . . Then as if at a given signal, the run of the smooth undulations seemed checked suddenly round the brig. By a strange optical illusion, the whole sea appeared to rise upon her in one overwhelming heave of its silky surface, where in one spot a smother of foam broke out ferociously. And then the effort subsided. It was all over, and the smooth swell ran on as before, in uninterrupted cadence of motion, passing under us with a slight friendly toss of our boat. Far away, where the brig had been, an angry white stain, undulating on the surface of steely grey waters shot with green, diminished softly without a hiss, like a patch of pure snow melting in the sun. . . . 'Gone!' ejaculated from the depths of his chest my bowman in a final tone. He spat on his hands and took a better grip of the oar.'

This incident made a profound impression on the young Conrad. It was not so much the loss of a gallant ship that roused his bitterness and indignation, as the prolonged strain, the cat-and-mouse cruelty that had robbed her crew of their courage and human dignity. 'Just as the sun went down,"' the captain told him, 'the men's hearts broke. They told me the brig could not be saved, and they thought that they had done enough for themselves. I said nothing to that. They lay about aft all night, as still as so many dead men.' There was more – much more – and Conrad never forgot it. 'I saw the duplicity of the sea's most tender mood . . .', he writes. 'I had looked coolly at the life of my choice. Its illusion had gone, but its fascination remained. I had become a seaman at last.'

The fascination remained. But we are land creatures, and when from the safety of the shore we allow ourselves to admire the strength and beauty of the sea, we cannot help knowing that the strength is hostile and the beauty alien. The dwellers in the deep, from Leviathan to the minute organisms that stain or illumine the waters, are strange and remote from us. They may be frightful as the medusa, or lovely as the glimmering fishes of the abyss; they may be warm-blooded and suckle their young, but they are not of our world. Seals

* *I.e.* on the night before the rescue.

are no longer believed to be human beings under enchantment; but the modern naturalist has not lost his sense of wonder, of awe in face of their mysterious aloofness. We look down on them from cliffs, as they play in spumy surf or marbled swell, and know that no human swimmer could live in such waters, or enter their circle except as a corpse, drifting and swaying with the tides. To watch the Atlantic seals in their own place, as I have often seen them in Barra, in waters where outlying skerries break the full force of the great waves, is to realise the alien, terrifying background of the old seal stories. Tales of men and women under spells, with personality intact, living as seals, and forced at certain times to go ashore and to stay at human hearths with human loves, till the day came for them to resume the wet, silky skin and go back to the sea whence they came. In concert hall and drawing-rooms, adorned with modern accompaniments and sentimental English translations, the Hebridean seal songs have become mildly romantic, almost domesticated, and the wild disquieting note is almost silent. But in the isles themselves, in the uproar of winter storm or under the searching gleam of lonely stars, we may thank God that no seal-woman is at our hearth, even as we thank Him for having spared us the foreknowledge of the next drowned man to be found in the tangle at dawn.

The fascination of the sea was strong enough to draw a Polish lad from the heart of a land without a coast, and make him take the life and language of an island race. It has been strong enough to set the creative imagination to work on subjects in which the sea itself is protagonist. We have outgrown the fashion of personifying the forces of Nature, but they have lost nothing by being allowed to appear in power and terror naked and unadorned. I am thinking especially of *Riders to the Sea*. J. M. Synge died young, leaving six plays, of which this one-act tragedy is the best; and even had he lived to fulfil his promise, I doubt if he would have written anything finer. His work for the Irish drama did not begin at once. Like many a young man of letters, he went abroad: and it was Yeats who found him writing in a garret in Paris, and sent him home to live among the people of Aran and discover the riches of his own country.

In the early years of this century the Aran Islands were still beyond the pale of material civilisation, and the Gaelic revival which brought so many scholars and students to this stronghold of the ancient tongue was then only in its beginning. If, outside Ireland, you spoke of Aran, you were supposed to mean Arran of the excursion steamers. But things are different now. The bounds of the unknown have contracted and films and stories have made the life and background of the islanders familiar to thousands who have never set foot in any part of Ireland. The place where Synge learned his craft is no more than a group of rocks in the Atlantic, without trees, almost without soil, except that which men have made from seaweed and rocky detritus carried up in creels. Fishing and local transport is still done in lath-and-canvas canoes, the direct descendants of the coracles in which the Irish saints went forth upon their missionary journeys. If Aran were made of gneiss or Torridonian sandstone, it would hardly support human life. But these rocks are of limestone, so kindly to stock; and the young beasts reared there are eagerly sought after on the mainland. Yet for all that the sea is master. The men of Aran must get their main living from the deep, and the sound of the surf, at all times circling the isles with its haunting music, is the background of that life which Synge, as far as he could, was to make his own.

As far as he could. For an island community is complete in itself. Bound by the closest ties of kindred, by hardship and danger shared, deeply religious, profoundly conservative, it forms a guarded circle into which it is almost impossible for a stranger to penetrate. Synge lived among the people, gained their confidence, learned their language. He was happy and well-liked; but there must always have been something alien and remote about him, if it were only the thorny aloofness that often hedges the artist. He did not share their religion, he had never looked hunger in the face, nor known, as far as we can tell, the depths of personal grief and loss. In a curious revealing passage of his book on the Aran Islands he describes his sense of loneliness, of apartness when the family he lived with had all gone to Mass, and he was left alone in the house.

But there is one point at which, by the sheer force of creative imagination, Synge was able to break down the barriers. *Riders to the Sea* is his finest play, and the only one that deals directly with Aran. The first idea of it may have come to him at an island funeral, where the wild, defiant keening of the women seemed less an expression of personal grief than the protest of all mankind against the sea's 'unfathomable cruelty'. Hence the universal note which, in its directness and poetic beauty, lifts *Riders to the Sea* to the level of Greek tragedy.

The play is very short. Every word counts, and it moves without a flaw to its predestined end. There is nothing in it but the age-long struggle between man and the sea, and mother-love pitted against the lust for adventure, necessary to life and in itself alluring, that must lead at last to the 'pasture of seals' and women keening in the night. As Cathleen says, 'It is the life of a young man to be going on the sea,' and it is also the life of the old to be waiting for those who return no more. Outside the cottage the wind is rising, and the noise of the sea increasing from moan to roar: within we hear the voice of the old woman Maurya as it moves from defiance to acquiescence. She has already lost her husband and four sons, and of the survivors, one, Michael, has been missing too long for hope. The new boards for his coffin are seen leaning against the wall.

The curtain rises on the two daughters, Cathleen and Nora, secretly opening a bundle of clothes found on a drowned man, which are believed to be Michael's, and are presently identified. The youngest boy Bartley is proposing to take a mare and pony to Galway Fair. The hooker in which he is to cross is already nearing the harbour, but a storm threatens, and the old woman vainly tries to keep him back. He makes a halter for the mare of a rope hanging beside the planks, changes his shirt for a newer one belonging to Michael, and goes out. He forgets to take his 'piece' with him, and Maurya runs out with it, to intercept him as he passes the spring well. After a while she returns, and tells the girls how she saw Bartley pass on the mare, and the grey pony following behind, with Michael on its back, in his best clothes, with new shoes on his feet. 'It was not Michael you seen,' Cathleen exclaims, 'for his body is after being found in the far north.' But her words mean nothing, for she knows as well as her mother who was the rider on the grey pony.

In times of vision or great emotion, the boundaries of time and space are merged into a continuous here and now. We hear the old woman recalling the day when Patch was drowned, and she sat at the same hearth with the child Bartley on her knee. Women came in threes and fours, silently crossing themselves, and kneeling to keen: and after them, men carrying a burden wrapped in a sail, which made a trail of drops in the dust at the door. No sooner has she spoken than a noise is heard outside, and women come in, and then men, with Bartley's body between them. They tell her that the grey pony knocked him off the rocks, and he was swept out to sea in the backwash of a wave. It is then that Maurya, with the last of them gone, makes her great speech. 'They are all gone now and there isn't anything more that the sea can do to me. . . . I'll have no call now to be up crying and praying when the wind breaks from the south, and I won't care which way the sea is when the other women will be keening. . . . It's a great rest I'll have now, and a great sleeping in the long nights after Samhain.'

There is here a mingling of two streams, the Christian acceptance of God's will, and the primeval fatalism of seafaring people, which finds expression in the Hebridean belief that the sea must have its own, and he who rescues a drowning man will bring the same danger on himself. Every word in the play, every action, is significant. Short as it is, and full of homely touches,* it is a complete vision of island life, with its struggles, forebodings, heroisms, and final acceptance. The old woman and her daughters are left alone, with no man to fish for them or work the croft. But the courage and human dignity – all that those Danish sailors had lost – is still intact; and in that wild place, with the sea at the door and the voices of wind and waves rising to storm, we know it is enough.

There is another book, coming from the other end of the Celtic world, in which the sea is also protagonist. It is hard to compare Pierre Loti's *Pêcheur d'Islande* with *Riders to the Sea*; for a novel, with its slower movement and more widely dispersed interest, could never achieve that closely knit unity. Once more we are confronted with the life and death of young men on the sea, and the tears and waiting ashore. We hear the same Atlantic surf beating on rockbound coasts, and see the unearthly gleam of Polar seas. Big Yann has a gayer, more defiant mood than the men of Aran, but is no less surely doomed. The book opens in the cabin of the *Marie*, darkened to exclude the pale dead rays of the midnight sun. Yann and his comrades are jesting about marriage. It ends with an unwitnessed struggle, on a day or night unknown, when the jester met his appointed sweetheart face to face, and endured the final embrace.

---

* See especially Bartley's parting instructions to his sisters, 'See that the sheep aren't jumping in on the rye'; the girls' talk about Michael's clothes; and the old man's remark, 'It's a great wonder she wouldn't think of the nails, and all the coffins she's seen made already.'

Loti was an officer in the French navy, which has always been largely recruited from Brittany, and he knew his Bretons. The love story of Yann and Marguerite is ostensibly the main theme; but it is not in them, but in the boy Sylvestre and in the heroic figure of the Widow Moan that Loti, like Synge, attains the fullness of vision. These two, in their tenderness and strength, their wisdom and dignity, have been moulded by hardship as stones are worn smooth by the waves. They belong not to Brittany only, but to all seas and desert places. Sylvestre is a naval conscript who escaped the storms of Iceland only to fall by a stray bullet in a skirmish in China. The Widow Moan is left, like Maurya, standing alone and undaunted in face of the sea that has taken everything.

I am churlish enough to wish that the book had been written in another tongue. Unequalled for logic or learning, for grace and wit, French is not the language of poetry or of prayer, nor can it quite adequately express men's deepest passions and aspirations. Every tongue, with the possible exception of Greek, has its limitations, and I cannot help thinking that *Pêcheur d'Islande* would be even better than it is had it been written in Breton, Gaelic, or English. France has its long Atlantic coast, and its sea-worn promontory in which a Celtic language still survives. But that language is not an indigenous survival, but an importation from Britain, and there is little in France today, or in the French tongue, to remind us of ancient Gaul.*

---

* Except those anomalous numerals – Roman from 1 to 79 and Celtic from 80 to 100. *Quatre-vingt*, so provoking to the Englishman, is familiar enough to Welsh and Gaelic speakers.

But we must not grumble. In the literature of the deep, *Pêcheur d'Islande* has its own place. From the first page to the last there is nothing in it but the sea and its influence on men. For all its cruelty and bitter deeds, it is the sea that has made our island people what they are. It is good for us to be in the presence of a friend whose changing face is ever the same, of an enemy whose worst furies are impersonal, of a force which makes us conscious both of the greatness of our daring and of the smallness of our power.

Man is born to wander. Physical movement and mental curiosity is his life, and there is no lasting rest for him on this side of the grave. Hence our delight in the making and using of roads. To sit by the evening camp fire, with a rich smell of frying in the air, and the sight of to-morrow's trail disappearing over the hill – what more could you ask? On a winter's night, if one had nothing better to do, it would be interesting to find out how large a part the simplest words connected with travelling – the word 'via' for instance, and its modern equivalents – have come to play in the vocabulary of civilised languages. But it is easier to start a hare than to find time to pursue it.

The simplest form of road is an animal's track on sand or snow, which has been followed by another beast for guidance, pursuit, or ease in travelling. It is fascinating to walk on freshly fallen snow or on the sands of a great ebb, and study the tracks of birds and beasts, so random as they seem to us, so purposeful as they are without doubt, if only we had the key. They are fresh too, for tracks in snow or loose sand are quickly drifted over, and the tale of the ebb renewed at every tide. Even the footprints of men – the grouping of tackets on shoes, the patterns on the soles of our gumboots, have their own story to tell, especially if our neighbours are few enough for us to recognise their footgear, and so be able to speculate about their business. It is fine to watch a dog trotting across the shore, spinning out a track behind him, as if he were a spider paying out gossamer. Or to examine our own footprints above the tide-mark, as they gradually lose their distinctness and finally vanish; for sand, like water, can keep no troth.

No one would believe how difficult it is, even when making direct for any given point over ground without obstacles, to keep in a straight line. The other day I had to cross Traigh Eais,* the only strand in Barra which can compare, in length and smoothness, with the great sands of South Uist. It is a flat expanse of sand, unbroken by rocks, bounded to the east by a line of high dunes, and to the west by waves breaking many rows deep on the gentle slope of the shore. Even with the horizon as a guide and example, I found that my trail, as I looked back on it, was anything but straight. Each turn of the head or sway of the body must have caused some slight deviation. They laugh at the roll of a drunken man or of a sailor ashore; but it would take a sober landsman all his time to walk mathematically across the sands. There is a tale told in the islands of a priest on horseback who met a drunken man zigzagging along the road. The priest told him to stand aside, but the fellow still had his wits about him, for he replied, 'But isn't it easier for yourself to keep out of my way than for me to keep out

---

* Traigh Mhor contains more square acres of sand; but facing away from the Atlantic, and being square rather than long, it comes into a different category. Traigh Eais is about 1½ miles long.

of yours?' A good story on the road; but it might not have been so apt on the sands.

The same thing happened when I laid out a footpath across a field we meant to enclose for hay. The course ran from gate to gate without obstacles to deflect a walker. I took what I believed to be the shortest line to the further gate, and paced across, leaving a paper trail to guide me, until the path should have become sufficiently trodden to be recognised at night. But that path when made was as crooked as a child's parting, without any reason for it. So that it is not remarkable if people walk in circles in woods or in thick darkness.

Animals travelling short distances on habitual business will leave a straight enough path, as I have noticed often enough when gazing sadly at the tracks of rabbits in standing grass. But where distances are greater and objects of fear or interest appear to divert the animal's attention, the ways become devious. Take a crofter's dog. All dogs are greatly dependent on having their interest held, and the crofter's collie, being chronically out of work, spends his life sitting on some eminence in the hope that something or someone will appear to bark at. Occasionally when bored beyond endurance, two or three of them go down to the shore by themselves; and their tracks, as they run about in search of diversion, form a labyrinth almost impossible to follow. If the course taken by a young dog, even when walking with its master, were plotted out, not only its length, but its variety would be beyond belief.

Except on paper, or on a featureless plain without

obstacles, the shortest road anywhere is not the straightest line, but the line of least resistance. Such a road is the quickest to travel and the simplest and cheapest to build. We can learn this much from water. A burn will find the easiest way down, and the hollow it scoops for itself from watershed to main valley becomes the pass followed first by pack-trains, and then by the modern road and railway. The movement of water, bound up as it is with our very life, is so sympathetic to us that it is not only children, or merely the child in grown-up men, that love to set it free. Draining is backbreaking work, but the moment when the stagnant water begins to run is worth it all. The long silence is broken; for from a dead swamp you have made a living stream. It is like letting a singing bird out of a cage.

Sheep are thought silly, but the paths they make on steep hillsides need not be despised by the engineer. However abrupt the slope, the track itself, compacted by the treading of countless hoofs, is always hard and firmly terraced. Rocks, bogs, and precipitous places are cleverly avoided, and the line of least resistance carefully followed. Burns are crossed at natural fords, where the widening of the channel makes the water shallow, the current weak, and the approaches easy and safe. The sheep's choice of a ford is sound, for lambs must be got across even in times of spate; and the engineer might do worse than follow it. The beginnings of these hill tracks are full of interest. You cross a slope covered with rough grass, sedge, heather, perhaps bracken, and there is nothing to be seen. Then you may notice a certain bending and bruising of the grasses, a broken twig and slight compaction of the soil, which can be felt as you walk. Little by little a definite path emerges, along which the poorer grasses give way to better varieties, perhaps to wild white clover; and this growth, which was originally stimulated by treading, attracts sheep to graze, so that there is more treading and more manuring; and in this way the sheep-paths improve the hill – a thing which the tarmac road will never do, however much we may squander the rates on it. The green sward and hard-packed soil of the track will often stop the advance of a heather fire, provided that there is not a strong wind to carry the flames across the gap.

It was once our business to start a new hill-track for the carting of milk-churns to the road where the lorry passed. The ground, though not steep, was full of rocks and stones too heavy to shift. For the sake of the precious milk we had to choose our road; and the trail of our wheels, as we dodged this obstacle or that, soon came to resemble a double sheep-path, for we had rubber tyres which left no ruts. At the end of a few weeks the new track had become part of the landscape, and could hardly be distinguished from others centuries old. But this bypassing of difficulties may be carried too far. I knew an old fellow who had a milk round in a neighbouring town. One day a tree blew down across his farm road – not a large tree, and full of good fuel. But sooner than saw it into handy lengths for carting, he let it lie, and drove round it, thus making a rutted track on the muddy ground at the side of the road. Truly the lazy man's burden!

The Romans made straight roads. But they had plenty of

slave labour; and the military authorities, confronted with the now familiar problem of keeping armies of occupation themselves occupied, must have thanked whatever gods there be for the forests and marshes of Gaul and Britain. The south and west of Ireland are covered with little roads leading nowhere in particular, built to give employment in the lean years. For the making of roads, and their upkeep when made, provide any amount of work, since Nature, with water and wind, with sand-drift and weeds, is for ever making war on them. And it is just in the remote and sparsely populated districts, where roads are least used, that their construction and repair are most difficult and expensive. In the Highlands, the engineer's chief obstacle is not forest or rock or water, but peat. A peaty surface will bear the traffic of horse and cart, but quivers like a jelly under the wheels of lorries. To clear away these immemorial deposits, till the firm bottom is reached, and fill up with hard material, is no cheap and easy matter.

Indeed, in the smaller islands, where the longest distance can easily be covered by ponies, and time and hurry do not exist, a modern tarmac road has not proved an unmixed blessing. Two years ago in North Uist, I heard men complaining that the new road had deprived them of the winter work they got in repairing the old one. In Benbecula people were grumbling at the proposed bridge across the South Ford, because when tradesmen's vans came over from South Uist, the isle would lose its ancient independence. In Barra, which is only six miles long, the new circular tarmac road proved a long and costly affair. Before the war, almost everything was transported by lorry, and the ponies ran idle. People were already complaining of the expense; and now that most of the lorries have been taken away, Barramen will find that a trip to the pier with pony and cart, for themselves or for a horseless neighbour, may be a welcome distraction in winter, especially in these days, when hardly anyone troubles to cart seaweed.

If you are on foot or on horseback, a long straight stretch of road is an abomination. Indeed I would almost say that a tired wayfarer will find a straight mile three times as long as a crooked mile. For the way to be travelled seems to reach to infinity, and distant landmarks appear to recede as the walker advances. People and animals are as dots growing gradually larger, until when you actually meet or overtake them, you are sick of the very sight of them. While on the winding road, these chance encounters come suddenly without warning; you move with ears pricked and mind alert. Each upward bend of an ascent may be the last, each figure stepping round a corner may be the one who has come to meet you.

If I could not have mountains or sea as a view from my window in old age, I would choose the sight of a road vanishing round a corner in woods, or disappearing over a pass of the hills. And it would need to be a road with a surface soft enough to show ruts and footmarks, and on it a homely plop of dung, and a few puddles to reflect the stars. What pleasure is there in the contemplation of a tarmac road, with nothing significant on it but white stripes and blobs of dirty oil?

Trailing nakedly across our green land, it reminds one of a strip of crude shiny linoleum, taken from the passage of a villa for the spring cleaning, and laid out flat on the daisies and dew of April.

There are several kinds of south-east wind, and every one of them unpleasant; for this wind is not a native of these islands, but an interloper from the Continent. Even on the west coast, where it comes offshore, it is cold in winter, parching hot in summer, and at all times devilishly persistent. For any east wind, no matter from what point or with what strength it blows, is always relentless; it moves not in gusts and lulls, but in one continuous blast. The sky may be cloudy or clear, but the south-easterly look is unmistakable. If overcast, the clouds are thick and murky, with a dark haze on the hills, and a short horizon, as if the whole world were burning heather. There will be livid gleams on loch and sea, and on the wide sands of machair and shore; and the following night is as dark as the pit. But if the sky be clear, you will see a sinister violet shade in the blue, and hard stereoscopic distances, very different from the crystal brightness of the north-west wind. The higher clouds are set in waves or lozenges, or packed into the curdled formation that heralds thunder. The sun often rises in wild and ominous redness; and in the Highlands there is nearly always an aromatic scent in the air, which many have noticed, but no one seems able to explain.

There are three main varieties of the south-easter: the wind which comes with the onset of an Atlantic depression at any season; the wind that blows from a continental anti-cyclone in winter, bringing a raw, cold, and often stormy weather; and the wind from the same source in summer, which struggles with the cool moisture of western air, and gives us thunder.

The first kind is no true south-easter, for it is only part of a travelling disturbance which begins with rain from the south-east and ends with hail or sleet from the north-west. Its force, and the pelting deluge it brings, can be truly appalling; but we can face it, for we know that before long it will veer south. As the driving rain crashes and splinters against the panes, and seeps in over the threshold, we learn that outside doors should never face this quarter, just as a bedroom for quiet sleep should look north, since northerly gales are rare. On the Atlantic coast it is, at least diagonally, a land wind, and can never reach the force of the south-west, or set in motion the same enormous waves. But in its mad rush down narrow glens it can play the deuce in a sea loch, and raise an ugly sea outside, if it happens to blow across a heavy westerly swell. It would strike full on the face of the jerry-built schoolhouse of Tanera, searching out the chinks and crevices of ill-fitting windows and doors, for no part of our immense education rates appear to be spent on honest joinery. The draught – if you can give that name to something that swings the heaviest curtain – was unequalled in the isles: you must either keep the inner door open, and shiver in the blast, or close it and listen to the relentless shriek of the keyhole.

The second variety of south-easter may come at any time in winter or early spring; and though the sky has often a most threatening appearance, there is no rain, or at most a few hard-wrung drops. I remember a day in December, when, as so often at Fernaig, I was busy carting wood. The sky was full of dark high clouds that streamed over the tops of the hills, and now and again let fall a spatter of drops. The iron-grey loch was scored with catspaws close inshore, for a big spring tide was at its lowest ebb, so that the edge of the water was well beyond the shelter of the railway embankment. Farther out, among the islands, were short snarling waves, capped with foam; and beyond them the gloomy hills of Applecross, wrapped in a murky smoke-like haze. The air was full of the sighing of pines and lashing of birches, and the peevish slapping of short waves among the skerries. Soon would begin a struggle with the doors of stable and byres, for a Highland steading is designed to give shelter from the west and south only. This south-east wind brings always to my mind things exasperating and uncomfortable – dust blowing and wisps of hay and straw awhirl, doors banging, windows rattling, heather fires out of control, cows calving in steep and awkward places in the woods. At the time of the heather-burning, smoke mingling with the natural murk would make the glen look like the outskirts of an industrial town.

The moonless nights of the south-easter can be very dark. One night in Barra I stepped out of the brightly lit schoolhouse of Craigston into a natural blackout, which, except for a ghostly glimmer on the sands and the breaking surf, was complete by land and sea. I could, by straining my eyes, just distinguish the white lines at the edge of the new road, but trusted mostly to the feel of the smooth surface under my feet. A little farther on, under the shoulder of Beinn Mhartuinn, the road, carried on an embankment, crosses a deep gully called Sloc a' Churaich, dividing it in two. The lower part is tidal, and at most times full of water left by the ebb. The upper end, now protected from the sea, is floored with rank grass and wild iris, and its rocky sides, sheer as the walls of a house, exclude the light of sun or moon. By the time I reached the Sloc – or rather the place where I thought it was, for there was no question of sight – the blanket of cloud fell thicker and lower. The tide was out, and the sea, dammed back by the east wind, was hissing softly on the sands. I did not like the sound of it, and swerving away from the outer curve of the road, I stumbled on the inner verge of rough grass. Recovering my balance, I remembered that there was no fence on that side of the embankment. Only a few days before I had been teasing a friend who did not care to pass the Sloc at night.

A strong south-easter raises a nasty sea in the Minch, and brings to the Western Isles the bitter breath of the mainland snow, not greatly tempered by so narrow a strait. On the Atlantic side of Barra it whistles down the glens of Craigston and Allasdale, driving cattle and ponies to shelter, and raising miniature sandstorms which run hissing across the machair, blurring the crest of every ridge, and drifting up whatever lies above the tide-mark. If there is no groundswell, the sea inshore will be calm, scored with darting catspaws like those we see on inland water, and fringed not with break-ing waves, but with seething, restless bands of froth. Farther out, beyond the shelter of the land, the leaden surface (for the typical south-easter robs everything, even the western ocean, of its colour) is gashed with white like the flash of fangs when a dog snarls suddenly. But if there comes a westerly swell, you will see the long slow waves, propelled by some force far beyond the range of this nagging wind, rolling on in spite of it, and breaking against it without effort, without hindrance, except that the crests are blown back like the streaming manes of galloping horses. The solemn roar of their advance is also blown backward, away from our ears, which are still full of the persistent scream of the wind. Should the sun appear, and colour come back to the world, the sight is not soon forgotten. The wrinkled sea far out is dark indigo verging almost on black, and slashed with the brilliant whiteness of foam; and the waves, breaking over golden sand, are all shades of blue-green, from the deepest peacock to the palest jade, where the westering sun strikes through the crests and turns the spray to a shimmering rainbow mist. In summer, and especially in July and August – for earlier in the season the winds are mainly from the north or west – the south-easter, blowing from the heart of a continental drought, gives us a hint of the parching heat of the desert. Dust, paper, wisps of straw and hay are lifted in the air, stooks fall without reason, trees, with their leaves turned back, rustle in fitful puffs, people are tired and peevish, boats on the choppy loch tug at their moorings.

I shall never forget one terrible day and night in Cornwall. It was late in July, and we had four acres of hay dry on the ground and ready for the rick. All day long the sun blazed down from a sky without cloud, without colour. The wind, which had been blowing freshly from the south-east since morning, rose rapidly to half a gale; and when we tried to load the hay it was torn from the forks and whirled away to leeward. The barometer was tumbling down, and we were clearly in for a storm, but what could we do? At sunset an ugly mass of cumulus heaved up from the south, but nothing happened except a steady increase of wind. Darkness fell, and one by one the misty stars were extinguished. So loud was the roar of the gale against the windows and in the sycamores, that for a long time it drowned the roll of advancing thunder. All night it blew and thundered and lightninged without intermission, with torrents of rain that flooded the fields of the valley. Our hay lay high and was safe, but it was some days before it was fit to handle, and it never recovered its quality.

I have never met anyone who had a good word for the south-easter, and I am sure that most of us would gladly see its lowering skies and hear its peevish voice for the last time.

Snow in its whiteness and silence is always uncanny, but never more than when it lies on sand at the fringe of ocean trodden only by birds, and the waves of the flood break on it in foam as white as itself. Deep snow comes rarely to the Western Isles, and the fall of mid-January 1941 was the heaviest for twenty-four years. First came showers, passing but thick enough in New Year's week, followed by a day or two of brilliant northerly weather, with an almost incredible clearness. From the slopes of Beinn Mhartuinn in Barra, every croft on the machair of South Uist, from Pollachar to far beyond Askernish, leaped to the eye, distorted and magnified by the refraction that in fine weather brings to the sandy island plains the illusions of the desert. I had not climbed very high before I saw, on the north-western horizon, what looked at first like a ship end-on under full sail, and then, as the morning sun shone more directly on it, like a great conical iceberg. To the left, a larger mass, also covered with snow, but less peaked, became visible and I knew that I was looking at St Kilda and the isolated pinnacle called Stac an Armuinn, which is the home of innumerable gannets. These isles are more than fifty miles away, and I was lucky to see them as I did, for small showers were trailing on the horizon, and before long one came and extinguished the vision.

That was the first snow. The second fall came later, and a strong north-east wind soon piled it into drifts. On the promontory of Borve, not more than a few feet above sea-level, the flat machair land is broken only by a few dunes and hollows, where sheep find shelter from the gales of winter. Luckily the flock had been moved elsewhere a few days earlier, for its accustomed refuges were soon blocked with drifts from six to eight feet deep. The snow was crisp and dry, and before long the wind had swept it from all exposed surfaces. You could see it streaming from the rocks into the sea to mingle with the spray, or drifting like mist round the summits of the hills, or running like blown sand on the surface of the machair. In the lee of the dunes, which the wind of ages had sculptured into fantastic curves, it lay heaped in coils and wreaths, but to windward the tough enduring sea-bent raised its tawny-gold spears. On the long windswept strand at Allasdale light powdery snow was ever on the move. As I stood back to the wind to get my breath, I was facing the sun, which hung low in the south-west, above the dark ridge of Ben Tangaval. The blown snow whirled and eddied under my feet in waving lines, and the level beams of the sun shone through it, as often it shines through the mist of spray over breaking waves, and turned it to stardust. At the water's edge the ebbing tide had left a strip of tawny sand between the snowy upper shore and the blue-green plains of the sea. A few stirks and Barra ponies, with the warm rich-ness of winter in their shaggy coats, were picking among the shining brown tangle, watched by seals swimming close inshore. Flocks of dunlins were busy among the froth at the fringe of the tide. A wedge-shaped flight of fifteen or sixteen geese passed away south. There were blobs of tar and crude oil on the rocks, half masked by the sand that stuck to them, and here and there lay the body of an oil-bound sea-bird, the war's most innocent victim.

Then came a day with a groundswell and clouds with soft melting edges, and I had a bet with a neighbour that a change of wind was coming. But the strange and lovely night that followed belied this hope; and for many another day the east wind so hated by islesmen persisted without a break. Not long before midnight I took the road from Craigston to Allasdale, which curves round the foot of Beinn Mhartuinn, skirting the rocks that separate the sands of Garriemore from Traigh Thamarra. There was no moon and the stars were not very clear, but behind the long promontory of Ardgreian the whole north-western quarter was aglow. There were three concentric arcs of light, of a colour whose richness and unearthly quality has no counterpart in Nature, and from the eastern end faint searchlight beams rose quivering to the zenith. Westward, dark anvil-headed snow clouds, blown to fantastic shapes by unfelt currents of air, lay motionless on the horizon. The auroral light was almost bright enough to cast a shadow, and it put a deep rosy glow on the snowy shore, and a paler shade of the same colour on the calm plains of the sea. There was a slight groundswell, and each wave, as it rolled shoreward and rose to break, seemed to pause for a moment, revealing the shadow under the crest along the whole length of the strand. Landward, the snowy summits of the central hills of Barra – Grianan, Corabheinn, and Harteval – melted into a sky in which was no darkness at all.

There were big drifts at the back of the house, which was sheltered from the east, and the hollow of the burn from which I drew my water was buried to a depth of several feet. There seemed no sense in digging it out, since it would soon be drifted over again; and profiting by my favourite Antarctic literature, I filled my pails with snow and set them to melt by the fire. At first a two-gallon pail would yield about a quart of water, but later, when the drifts packed hard, I could get twice that quantity. In spite of snow's apparent purity, this water always contained some of the ubiquitous sand of the machair. I pitied my friends on the mainland with their elaborate water systems, their vigils with lamp and stove, their fruitless appeals to plumbers. My only trouble was that the driftwood on the shore was completely buried. The crofters' cattle were kept in, except for a walk to the water, and their owners were in no hurry to rise to a world of snow and whistling wind. The snow disappeared very slowly, mostly by evaporation, for although the temperature rose to well above freezing point, that persistent east wind never shifted. A few small patches remained on the hillsides, like sheets on the bleach, and the drifts on the machair dwindled to heaps of snow and sand, resembling nothing so much as sugar mixed with rather pallid cocoa. The sky was covered with woolly clouds which broke in many a place to show a tract of blue, clear as the lochs of Uist in summer. The seas of Barra, when they lie shallow over sand, have a unique green colour, even under the leaden skies of an east wind. But now in the light that filtered through the parting clouds, the green became an iridescent jade, with gleams of silver and opal and mother-of-pearl, and the foam at the water's edge was as white as the snow that had gone. At the northern end of Allasdale strand is a ridge of sand thrown up by centuries of storm, and behind it a shallow trough. The flowing tide came brimming over the ridge in slow silky waves, and each wave, as it retired with a gentle hiss, left the trough full of water, which sank into the porous sand with the bursting of a thousand bubbles. Before the next wave spilled over the ridge, the sand of its crest dried bare as the shell of a boiled egg dries when lifted from the pan.

Beyond the ridge, a stream of fresh water meandered across the sand. Swollen by the melting of snow in the Glen of Cuier, it was now too deep to cross in shoes, and rolled turbidly down to the sea through a rocky passage so straight and uniform in width that it looked like the work of man. At high tide and in rough weather, waves rush up this channel, damming back the burn as they advance and letting it down in their retreat. There is something intriguing about these streams of the machair. They constantly change their course as well as their volume. They disappear into sand-banks, from which they emerge at a lower level in countless small rills, which spread across the wet sand of the ebb in beautiful fronded patterns. They carve deep gorges with sheer sides, which collapse at the least vibration. At low tide, when there is least disturbance from the sea, you can see little spates coming down every half-minute or so, in a rhythm that does not correspond with that of the waves. That this is no optical illusion is proved by the sudden babble of water that accompanies them. They may be caused by the collapse, somewhere upstream, of their sandy banks. For on these western machairs, sand, sculptured and drifted by waves and wind, is a great force; and while snow is watery and transient, the sand which underlies it and ultimately swallows it will endure as long as the sea itself.